The Complete OIL PAINTING Course

The Complete
OIL PAINTING
Course

CRESCENT BOOKS
NEW YORK

Executive Managers	Kelly Flynn,
	Susan Egerton-Jones
Compiling Editor	Jean Wetherburn
Art Editor	Hans Verkroost
Editorial Assistant	Fiona Thomas
Production	Peter Phillips

SPECIAL THANKS to St Martin's School of Art and Chelsea
School of Art for their kind assistance.

1986 Edition published by Crescent Books,
distributed by Crown Publishers, Inc.
Edited and designed by the
Artists House Division of
Mitchell Beazley International Ltd
Artists House
14–15 Manette Street
London W1V 5LB

An Artists House Book
© Mitchell Beazley Publishers 1982, 1983 and 1986

ISBN 0–517–61203–8

Typeset by Hourds Typographica Limited, Stafford.
Reproduction by la Cromolito s.n.c., Milan.
Printed in Portugal by Printer Portugesa, Sintra.

hgfedcb

CONTENTS

HOW TO USE THIS BOOK

Many people have the ability to paint – it is a question of developing the talent. This book will help, by showing you the methods and techniques you will need to achieve specific goals. By following its systematic instructions, step by step, you will learn how to develop your skills in a fascinating medium.

The book is divided into three main sections: on materials, on techniques and finally a reference section that includes advice on making and obtaining materials, and protecting and storing pictures. There is also a glossary to help you understand technical terms used in the book.

This book is designed to be read and studied at leisure to build up knowledge of the approaches, methods and techniques of oil painting. It can also be taken with you into the studio or on painting trips as an essential part of your painting kit, to be referred to as you work.

MATERIALS

Introduction	6
Canvas	8
Boards	10
Stretching canvas	12
Size	14
Primers	16
Brushes	18
Paints and mediums	20
Palettes	22
Easels	24
Preparing to paint	26

TECHNIQUES

Introduction	28
Brush marks	32
Colour wheel and Tonal Scale	36
Colour keys	38

The tonal painting	40
Colour behaviour	42
Toned grounds	44
Colour observation	46
Line	48
Shape and form	50
The balance of shapes	52
Format	54
Harmony and proportion	55
Investigating your subject	58
Starting on the canvas	60
Looking at the composition	62
Development	64
Restating and alterations	66
Composing a still life	68
Painting flowers	69
Painting the figure	72
Colour and form	74
Painting portraits	76

Scale and distance	80
The sketch book	82
Painting landscapes	84
Seascapes	90
Towns and buildings	92
Painting animals	96
Colour expression	100

REFERENCE

Introduction	104
Recipes and canvas care	106
Framing	110
Storage	112
Glossary	114
Index	116

MATERIALS

An understanding of the materials used in oil painting is very valuable. Oil paint is a versatile and beautiful medium for the artists, and knowing just what it can and cannot do will help you to exploit its potential to the full.

In this section you can learn about the pigments and other elements which make up the paints, tools of the trade such as brushes, knives, palettes and easels, the different kinds of painting surfaces and the best methods to use to prepare them.

Finally, there are chapters on how to set up your work area properly, and take the first steps in preparing to paint.

CANVAS

The word canvas can describe a finished oil painting as well as the material or "support" on which an oil painting is executed. This support consists of either canvas stretched over a wooden frame; panels of wood or board; paper or cardboard. The support carries a ground consisting of size (a glue which seals the surface) and primer (an undercoat onto which the paint is applied). The best woven canvas is linen, but for practice work or painting on a large scale, cheaper cotton canvas is acceptable.

Choosing canvas

Poor materials may have a dressing or filler which gives extra 'body' and weight.

Choose raw linen without knots, and cotton that has no rought flecks.

Broken or uneven weave, or too much stretch on the bias, is undesirable.

Buying canvas

If buying raw canvas to prime and stretch yourself, go to a reputable art supplier or, ideally, you might be able to find a sailmaker or canvas supplier who stocks a variety of grades and widths. Choose the width that will cut up with the least wastage for the size and shape you want to paint. Offcuts can be glued to hardboard. Avoid materials composed of mixed fibres such as linen/cotton which stretches unevenly. Good linen has a tight weave of even threads which will persist through several layers of paint and remain firm under the brush; on cotton the texture quickly becomes obscured and the surface rather flat. Ready-primed linen or cotton by the metre is reliable, comes in various textures, and is convenient and quite economical to stretch yourself.

Canvas on stretchers

Commercially primed, stretched canvas is consistently even in quality and quick to get started on.

However, once having acquired some skill, it may feel rather more greasy than the canvas you prime yourself, but this is a matter of taste. Price, and restriction to the available sizes and shapes, are other drawbacks. Oil- and acrylic-primed canvas come in a choice of grades. (The durability of acrylic primer under oil paint is still in doubt.)

Standard sizes range from 254 × 305mm (10 × 12in) to 1016 × 1524mm (40 × 60in) at intervals of 25 or 50mm. Large sizes are held rigid with crossbars.

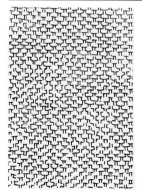

Tailor's canvas

Alternative supports

Any natural fabric, pale and unpatterned, such as worn linen, cotton tablecloths, muslin, or canvas offcuts can be glued to board. Tailors' canvas is a cheap, pure linen interlining.

Hessian has a dominant texture and needs much sizing. Old canvases are fine to paint on if scraped down.

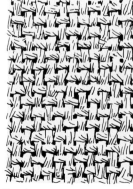

Hessian

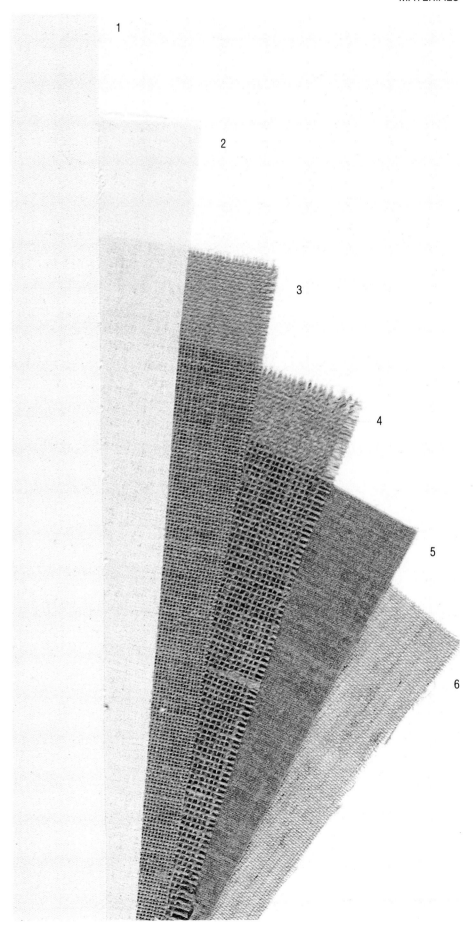

Six different types of canvas suitable for oil painting: white cotton duck (1), calico (2), fine jute screen (3), coarse jute screen (4), fine linen (5), fine linen scrim (6).

Linen canvas has a natural colour, whereas cotton is white or very light. Cotton has drawbacks: it fluctuates in tension in humid or dry condtiions, and stretches much more than linen. it is less tough, rots faster, and many painters consider it less responsive than canvas. Although linen is the best support, many people start off with primed cotton on stretchers; it is quite adequate and cheaper for experimenting. Linen and cotton are available in various weaves and qualities, in three states: raw (unprimed), ready-primed in rolls, and primed on stretchers. Textures range from fine to coarse. When choosing texture, weigh up factors such as the subject, its scale, how you will apply the paint, and what you best *like* to paint on. Coarse canvas has a better 'tooth' to anchor pint applied thickly wtih a knife, but if you use a sable brush and build up with tiny brushstrokes choose a fine exture, since coarse canvas would swallow up the paint.

BOARDS

Mahogany, for centuries the traditional wooden support, can no longer be relied upon to be well seasoned and not to warp, and is now so expensive that it has been superseded by a large number of more economical wood or composition boards. These can be painted on direct or covered with a plain natural material, and are usually primed with either gesso, with an egg emulsion, or with an oil undercoat. Paper has been used as a support since 1400; cardboard panels of paper pulp, or combined with wood or cloth, date back to the sixteenth century.

Examples of different boards:
Top left: hardboard
Top right: oil board
Below left: blockboard
Below right: Sundeala

Preparing boards

On paper, card or wood panels the image can grow in any direction, to be centred and trimmed later. White card or paper is sized only.

Coloured panels are sized, then painted on direct as a toned ground or given a thin coat of white primer.

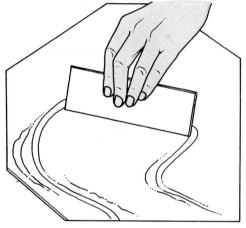

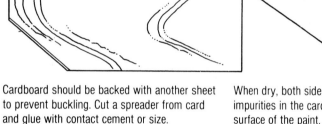

Cardboard should be backed with another sheet to prevent buckling. Cut a spreader from card and glue with contact cement or size.

When dry, both sides of the panel must be sized to prevent impurities in the cardboard persistently rising through to the surface of the paint.

Battening hardboard

Normally the frame will prevent a medium-sized board from warping or twisting. Sometimes you can simply choose a heavier board. Generally, panels of more than 75 × 100cm require bracing with seasoned wood, and you may also have to add a crossbar for ridigity.

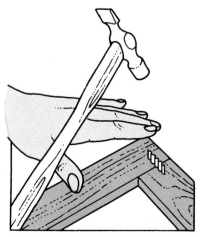

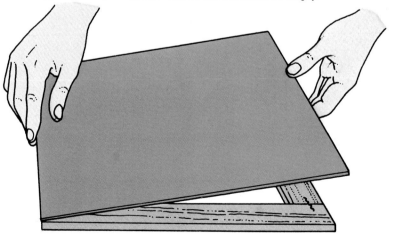

1 Cut four lengths of 25 × 50mm wood to the same dimensions as the panel. Join them up.

2 This frame can be either be glued to the wrong (ie textured) side of the board with strong adhesive (even after you have painted on it) and clamped, or tacked on with panel pins.

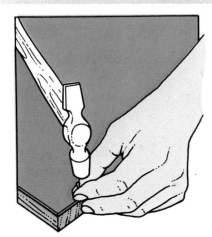

3 Drive in the pins at 5cm intervals around the perimeter of the right side of the board.

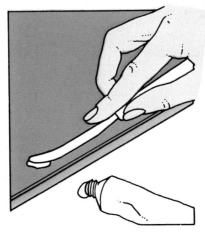

4 Countersink the holes and fill with plastic wood. You may have to do this twice.

5 When the filler is dry, sand the edges and the shiny surface to give a tooth for the size.

STRETCHING CANVAS

The bigger the canvas the stronger the stretcher you need. 609 × 914mm will need a stretcher with crossbar; 914 × 1219mm requires a double crossbar. There is usually a sharp edge and a bevelled edge to the outside of each piece. Make sure all four bevels face in the same direction, otherwise the sharp edge is likely to cut the cloth.

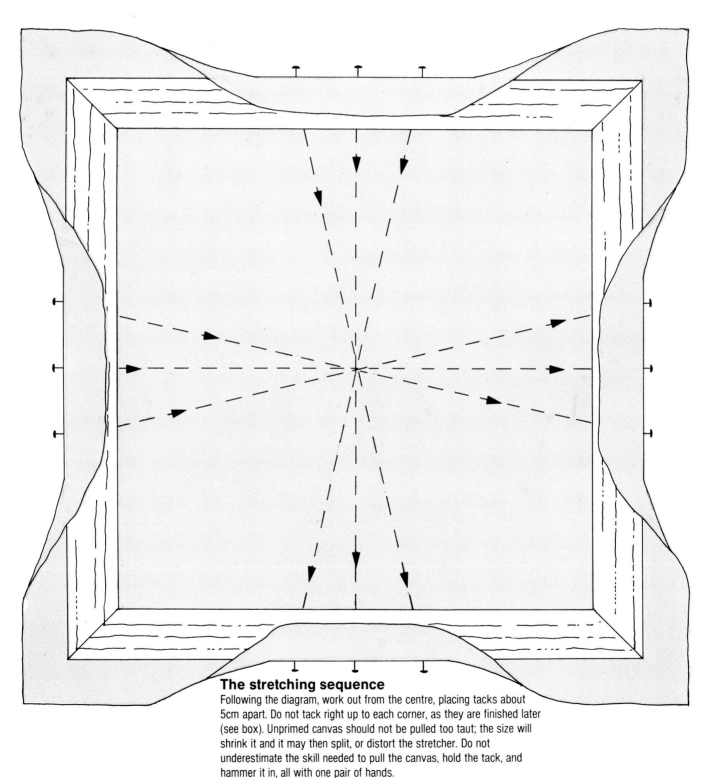

The stretching sequence
Following the diagram, work out from the centre, placing tacks about 5cm apart. Do not tack right up to each corner, as they are finished later (see box). Unprimed canvas should not be pulled too taut; the size will shrink it and it may then split, or distort the stretcher. Do not underestimate the skill needed to pull the canvas, hold the tack, and hammer it in, all with one pair of hands.

Stretching unprimed canvas

Is the stretcher square and true? Measure the diagonals with a length of string. If they are equal, the frame is square. A set square ensures precision but a rough check can be made by placing the stretcher on the corner of a table. Assemble the canvas, craft knife, steel ruler, hammer and steel tacks. (A heavy duty staple gun is effective when stretching canvas alone or when stretching a very large canvas.) Place the frame, bevelled side down, on the linen, aligned with the fabric grain. With the knife, cut the cloth 6cm larger than the stretcher on all four sides.

Assembling the stretcher

Push each mitred joint together, the bevelled edge uppermost. Tap the corner gently with a piece of wood or a mallet for a snug fit. Once correctly assembled, mark the joints in pairs of letters: AA, BB, CC, DD, in case the stretcher is re-used.

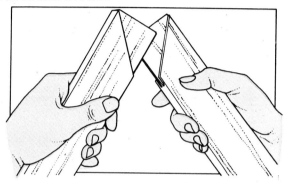

With the stretcher upright, fold the material over and, leaving tacks halfway in to allow for adjustments, drive in the first one in the centre of a long side, pulling the canvas firmly and evenly; it must stay square with the wood. Tack on each short side.

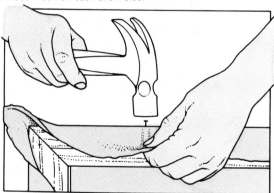

Stretching primed canvas

Primed canvas is less flexible than raw, and requires a special tool – pair of canvas pliers. Choose a piece of blemish-free, ready-primed canvas. Following the method for raw canvas, cut it out and attach it to the stretcher. Pull quite hard as it will not shrink in sizing, but take care not to crack the ground. Canvas pliers give the extra purchase on the material; a staple gun is an advantage if attempting the job alone.

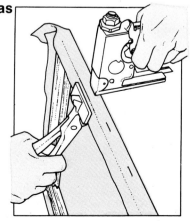

Handling the corners

1 Pull the cloth across the corner of the stretcher

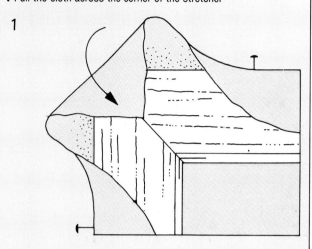

2 fold in each side of the cloth smoothly and neatly and **3** tack down both flaps. Finish the other corners, putting in the final

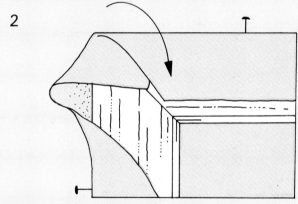

tacks about 2.5cm from each mitred joint, through the thickest part of the wood to prevent it splitting. Drive all the tacks home. Now lodge two wedges or keys temporarily in place in each corner: the longest side lies along the wood of the stretcher. If they are put in the wrong way round, they will split when hammered in against the grain. Do not drive them in tight for at least a year after the picture is finished as it will take this long for the paint to dry, and only then if the canvas becomes slack. Cotton is likely to need constant adjustment but linen remains taut.

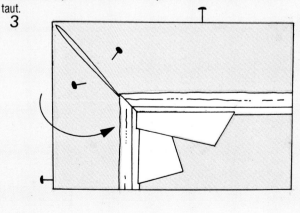

SIZE

Stretched canvas, board and other supports must be sealed before being used. The traditional method is sizing and priming. Size acts as a separating membrane to prevent oils seeping down and "rotting" the canvas, leaving the paint impoverished and eventually flaky. Apply two coats of size before priming, to discourage impurities from rising through to the paint, or damp penetrating from the back. Rabbit skin glue, available in crystals, granules or sheets, best combines flexibility with sealing qualities. It is important **not** to size the canvas if you are going to use an acrylic ground (see p16).

Preparing size

1 Put one rounded tablespoon of crystals into a 450g jam jar and let the contents soak in enough water to cover for about 20 minutes, when it will have doubled in bulk.

2 Fill the jar three quarters full of cold water and stand it on a lid or trivet in a saucepan of warm water.

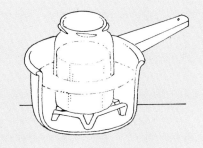

Sizing and preparing hardboard

Sand the shiny side and size both sides. Dry flat, then apply a second coat. It can either be primed (p106), or covered with fabric before priming.

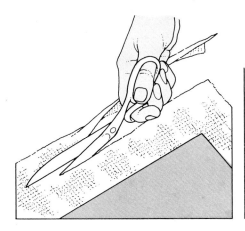

1 Take a sanded panel that is cut square and true and lay it down on top of the clean material. Cut a margin 5cm larger all round than the board. Trim off any loose threads.

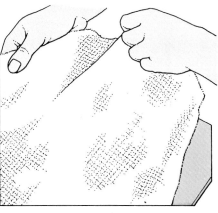

2 With lukewarm size and a household paintbrush, size the right side of the board, then smooth the fabric over it, keeping the weave parallel to the edge.

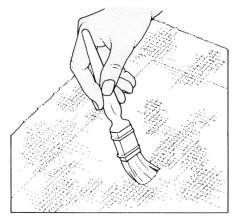

3 Now apply more size to the cloth, brushing from the centre outwards, working out any creases or bubbles. Keep the weave square or it will be very distracting when painting.

Sizing canvas

Dissolve jelly by standing the jar in a pan of water over low heat. Apply size lukewarm with a 38mm brush to the right side of the canvas, starting on the short side. Work from the edge in one direction only. Smooth the glue uniformly over the surface, including the edges. Keep the brush loaded but do not scrub it in or pile it on. If the size is too hot or is pushed in, it will form small bubbles or pinholes and soak through; if it is too strong, the ground will crack. Leave the first coat to dry for several hours, lying flat. Brush on the second coat in the opposite direction. As it dries, run a palette knife around once or twice between stretcher and canvas to make sure that they do not stick together. Wash the brush in warm water after each coat.

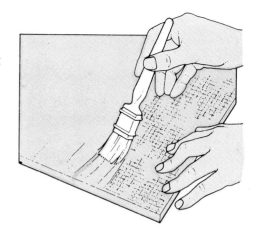

3 Dissolve the crystals over a gentle heat for about 30 minutes, stirring occasionally and never allowing the size to boil or the pan to go dry. You could also heat it in a coffee tin standing in water or in a double boiler, but in a glass jar you can see when the crystals have dissolved.

4 Let the size cool, forming a jelly. Don't stand it in cold water to do this or the jar may crack. Test it with a finger – you should just be able to break the surface, and it should not fall out if the jar is inverted. If too solid, reheat the size, add water, and allow it to reset.

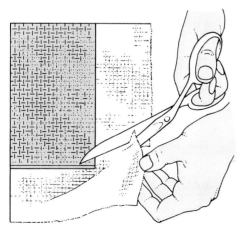

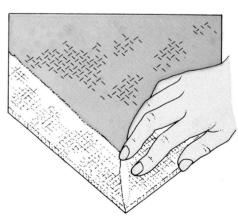

4 Turn the board and fabric over and trim across the corners, not cutting it too short as the size will shrink the material, nor leaving it too long as it will be lumpy in the frame.

5 Size a margin around the edge of the reverse of the board wide enough to stick down the overlapped cloth, which should not be pulled too tight as it encourages the board to warp.

6 Smooth down the flaps of material and fold the corners over neatly. Turn the board over, brush off any dust, and dry flat. Add a final coat and dry overnight before priming.

PRIMERS

The different types of ground vary in absorbency, and you will need to find out from experience which primer best suits your painting method. On a non-absorbent ground the paint remains fluid and can be pushed around easily. On a more absorbent surface the paint becomes matt and dry almost immediately, giving a flat, chalky quality. The simplest ground on canvas consists of two coats of size and a thin coat of housepainter's matt white oil undercoat. You can also lay a ready-made primer onto a board without sizing. The egg emulsion below is suitable for boards or canvas.

Other types of primer
Gesso: for panels only

Gesso with oil: for panels and canvas

Acrylic primer: a modern equivalent for wood or canvas supports.

Quality oil undercoat: a matt-drying, oil-based primer

Mixing an emulsion primer
This is the most versatile, reliable, whitest and longest-lasting painting surface. For a more absorbent ground, lay two coats; for less absorbency, apply up to four thinner coats, sanded between each one. Ingredients: 450g titanium white powder, a 50g (medium) egg, refined linseed oil and size. As a guide, this amount will cover two 50 × 60cm supports with three coats.

1 Break the egg into a jar with a tightly fitting screw top. Crack the shell evenly in half, as this is your measure.

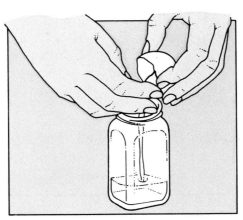

2 Fill each half eggshell with cold water twice, pour into the jar and shake. Fill each half eggshell once with linseed oil and add.

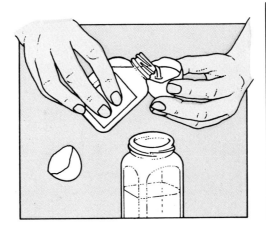

Laying the primer
With a household paintbrush, begin at the edge, brushing quickly evenly and thoroughly in all directions. While this dries (about an hour) the unused primer will solidify. Warm it again for the next coat and if too thick, add a little water. Lightly sand after each coat, applying three in all, drying flat in a clean place. Wash the brush in lukewarm water. Although the canvas can be painted on next day, it is much nicer if matured for six months.

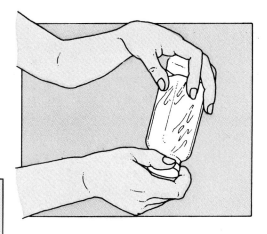

3 Shake hard for five minutes to emulsify. Stand the jar of size in a pan of warm water and melt the size over a gentle heat.

Traditionally gesso was a primer for tempera, gouache and oil, made up of size and slaked plaster of Paris, not size and whiting as it is today; the term is not now strictly accurate. it is a simple, reliable, chalky surface with no flexibility as it contains no oil so it is suitable only for boards. At least two coats are needed. If you find this ground too absorbent, add a final coat of size. it can be painted on next day. Unlike the egg emulsion, it does not improve with age.

Adding some linseed oil to the size and whiting recipe produces a slightly yellow ground which is flexible enough to be used on either board or canvas.

Bought ready-made, it must never be used over a sized support as it will crack badly. Apply one or two coats direct to the panel or canvas. The first one diluted with water by half the amount of the primer. Sand in between each coat with fine sandpaper. The surface can feel 'plastic' and durability is still to be proved.

Available from the hardware store, or as a prepared oil primer from art suppliers. Will yellow 'in time'.

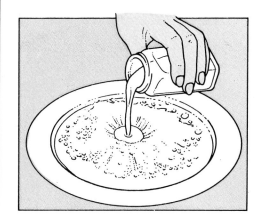

4 Place a third of the powder on a large plate, and make a well in the centre. Dribble in the emulsion, blending with a palette knife.

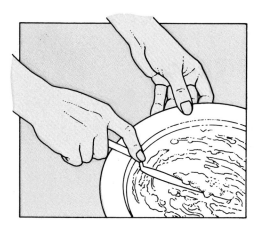

5 Smooth out all the lumps, slowly adding the emulsion until the mixture resembles thick cream cheese. Tip this into a bowl.

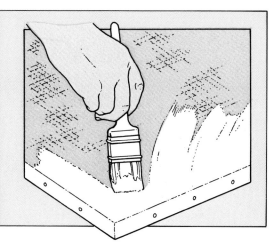

6 Add lukewarm size by degrees, stirring until it looks like thin cream. You can adjust the amount of size for the required absorbency.

BRUSHES

Brushes are one of the painter's major investments. When painting, each new colour demands a clean brush, and only good quality brushes will help you to apply the paint as you want to. The best brushes for oil paints are the stiff-bristled hog and the soft-haired sable, although brushes in many other materials are available. However, remember that brushes are not the sole tools you can use for applying paint; you may want to use your fingers for blending edges, or a painting knife for laying in thick colour.

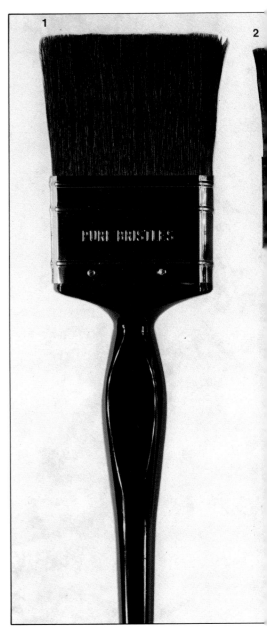

Worn brushes

A new brush will need several hours of use before it is "broken in". It should then wear evenly all round, keeping its shape, with no stray hairs. The two brushes shown on the left below are useful worn brushes, but the others are examples of badly worn brushes which should not be used. Makes vary in size, the amount of bristles and wearing qualities. Expensive sables can last 20 years, while cheap synthetics may survive for only a few painting hours. Lazy cleaning, harsh painting surfaces and messy painting habits will destroy any brushes in a matter of a few days.

The range of brushes

Household paint or varnish brushes (**1,2**) are useful for applying grounds and varnish. The best bristle brushes for oil painting are made from bleached hogs' hair, increasing in size from 1 to 12. Extra large sizes extend up to no. 36. Beginners should start off with sizes 2, 3, 5 and 6. Brights (**3-7**) and flats (**9**) can make monotonous brush marks, so you may be better to go for the round or filbert shapes (**8, 10**). Choose short or medium length bristles, as long bristles can be hard to control. Top quality sables (**11, 12**) are for finely detailed work, but take care to avoid fussy painting.

Cleaning brushes

1 The quickest way to shorten the life of a brush is to leave it dirty after use and then have to resort to paint remover to clean it.

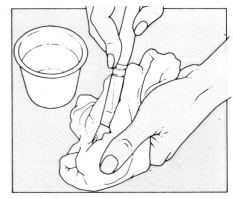

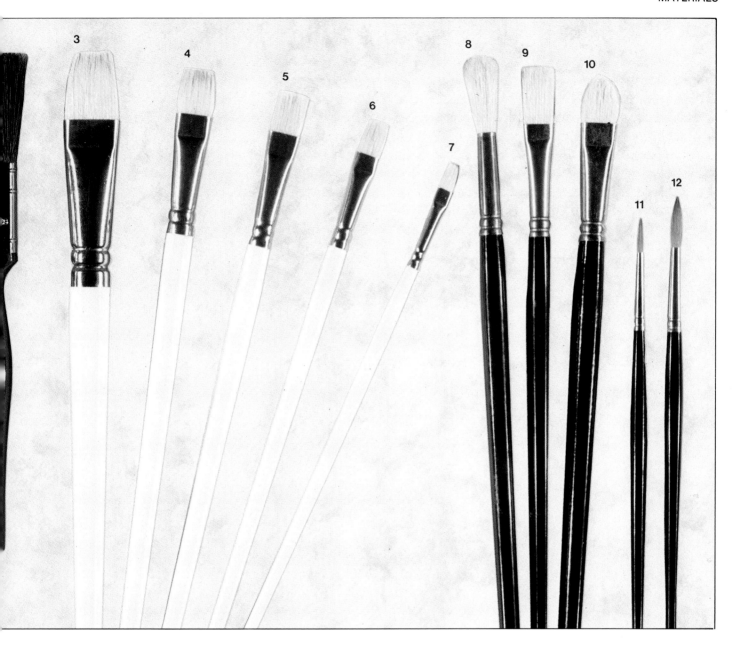

2 After rinsing in white spirit and wiping thoroughly on the rag, soap the bristles well with plenty of pure household soap and warm water.

3 Now rub the brush around gently in your palm, rinsing now and then, making sure that all the paint is out, especially around the ferrule.

4 Rinse the brush under warm running water, shake it out and smooth it into shape. (Don't get into the habit of licking brushes.)

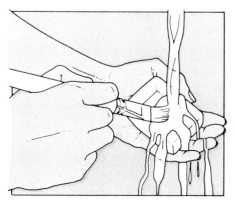

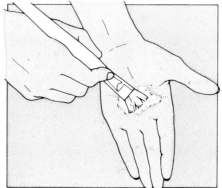

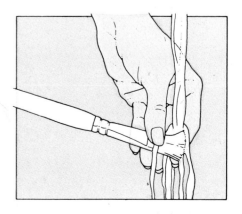

PAINTS AND MEDIUMS

When buying paints, the plain fact is that you get what you pay for. It is best not to economize, so buy the best you can. There are two ranges: the artists' paints are made in a wide range of pigments, regardless of cost; the students' or budget range offers a narrower selection from the cheaper, chemically based dyes, hence light-fastness is not as good. Paints vary in texture, opacity, degree of colour and adhesive permanence, depending on the chemical make-up of the pigment and the oil content. White and the earth colours (ochres, umbers, siennas) are generally thicker and more opaque than the darker paints like alizarin, ultramarine and black. It is these qualities which determine how and when they are best applied to the support.

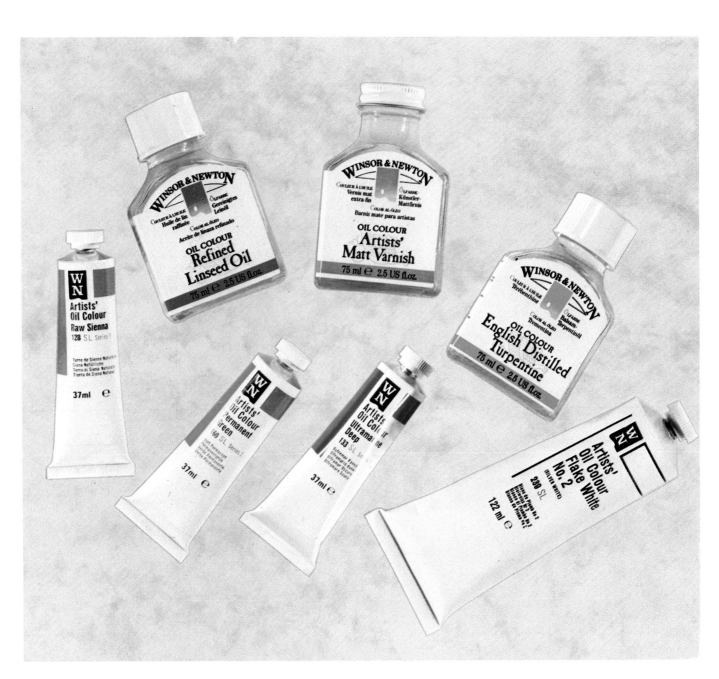

Caring for your paints

Colours tend to solidify in the tube if left uncapped. Put the cap back the moment you have used the paint, make sure the threads on cap and neck remain clean. A palette knife held at an oblique angle and scraped along a finished tube will remove the last scraps of paint.

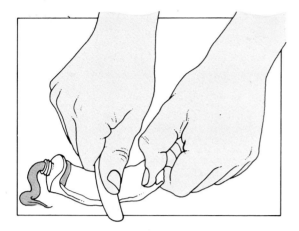

Stuck caps

If pliers do not work, hot water often will. Failing this, hold a match under the cap for ten seconds, or grip the cap between a door and the jamb, then twist if off.

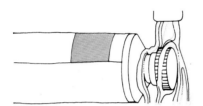

Removing excess oil from paint

Some colours contain more oil than others, and although this excessive oiliness can be blended with the paint when it is on the palette, it is sometimes more than you want to have to work with on the canvas. Squeeze some pigment on to a thickness of newspaper and leave it for a time. Some surplus oil will then be absorbed. This was often practised by artists such as Degas and Toulouse-Lautrec.

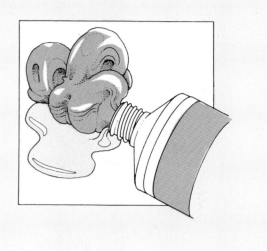

Mediums

There are many oils, diluents and varnishes that, when combined with the pigment straight from the tube, can be used to change its consistency: its "feel", its "fatness", plasticity and drying speed, so that the paint can be termed "short", "long" or even "buttery". Oil binds the raw pigment, adding more oil or more diluent alters its structure, character and handling, and ultimately the quality of the paint on the canvas. Finding which mixture suits your style or creates the effect you want to achieve can only be accomplished by trial and error. You may want to try using no medium at all, it is by no means mandatory.

After underpainting with paint and pure turpentine only, you could start with a medium of 15% refined linseed oil and 85% turps. As the painting builds, add an increasingly greater proportion of oil, but never more than one third oil to two thirds turps. This is called painting "fat

over lean", a sound old principle (p60). Experiment with mediums with varying drying speeds of viscosity and keep a record of the results in a note book. Once you have found a medium that suits you mix up a large quantity in a jar.

Keep the medium in the dipper clean and change it if necessary. Don't rinse your brush in it as it will make subsequent mixtures muddy and dingy. Colours should stay clear and bright. Refined linseed oil is a popular medium in combination with genuine turps (spirits of turpentine), with average drying speed and minimal yellowing. Linseed-based stand oil and sun-thickened oil mixed with turps are also quite common (p107). Genuine turps will evaporate and thicken unless kept closed and away from light. Use it for thinning down paint; rinse brushes in cheaper turps substitute (white spirit).

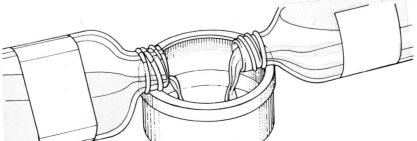

Warning: Don't leave paints within range of children. Flake (lead) white is dangerous, so do not let it get into a cut or under the fingernails. Wash your hands after painting.

PALETTES

If you rest your palette on a table, you can use any piece of smooth wood or glass. Otherwise, choose the studio shape (1), well balanced for standing at an easel, or the rectangular (2), which fits into a painting box and is good for outdoors. Paper palettes (3) in tear off pads, each used once, are less satisfactory. Use as large a palette as you can, to hold squeezes of pigment around the edge and generous mixtures in the middle, without all intermingling.

Making your own palette

Scale up the drawing on brown paper to make a template (one unit equals 3cm), or make one from a friend's palette, after trying it for size. A timber merchant will cut the pattern out of 5mm marine or Gaboon ply. Make sure that the best side will be uppermost. Sandpaper the edges, bevelling the thumbhole on the leading edge on

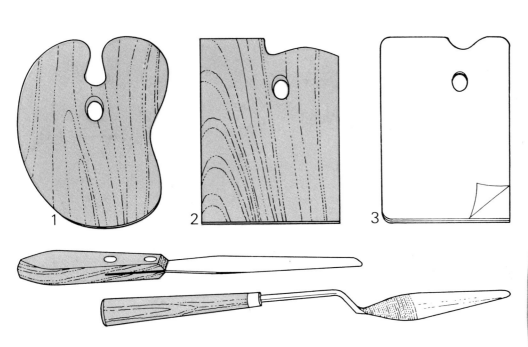

Knives

Painting and palette knives come in many shapes and sizes. **Palette knives** (top) are for drawing colours together, for losing an edge, for scraping off the paint (see p35). Some people use them for mixing paints on the palette, others favour brushes. They are handy for cleaning the mixtures off the palette at the end of the day and for transferring unused blobs of paint to an airtight tin. You can also apply paint with them, although cranked-handled **painting knives** in trowel, pear and diamond shapes are specifically designed for this purpose.

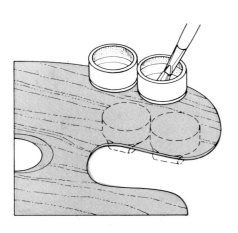

Dippers

Dippers clip on to the palette in the most convenient position. One holds medium, the other white spirit for rinsing brushes, but most painters who stand at the easel keep a glass jar or tin can on the painting table. If painting fluidly and using a lot of medium, or outside, or on holiday, pre-mix medium separately and pour a small amount into the dipper. Buy single dippers, with double dippers you cannot pour back the medium.

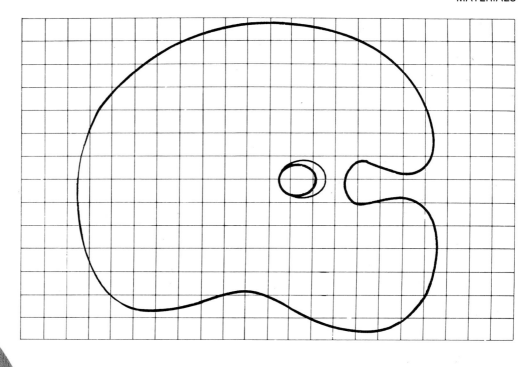

top and the back edge underneath. (Reverse for a left-handed palette.) Having adjusted the balance (right), season the wood several times with linseed oil overnight (this also applies to a bought one). The cost? About half those in the shops, and enough wood left over for a rectangular one too.

Holding the palette

Hold a kidney-shaped palette in the left hand (if right-handed), resting it on the forearm and fitting it up against your body. The bevelled edge of the thumbhole will be on the right side on top and on the left side (towards your left elbow) underneath. You may need to sand it to fit your hand. Can you hold the brushes comfortably in your hand, not in your fingertips? Check the balance of the palette by weighing it on your arm. A block of wood or lead weights can be fastened underneath; any imbalance will tire your arm.

Cleaning the palette

At the end of each painting session, scrape off the mixtures with a knife on to newspaper and wipe the palette with kitchen paper. If resuming in a day or two, the squeezes of pigment remaining can be covered with foil or a hard skin will soon make the paint lumpy. If not painting again for some time, these must be removed too. Now rub any oil/turps medium left in the dipper over the palette with kitchen paper or rag until clean – a wonderful patina will form in time. White spirit can be used also but is less beneficial alone and should be followed with a film of linseed oil.

EASELS

The adjustable studio easel (1) is expensive and cumbersome but ideal for large canvases. The compact radial easel (opposite) is more popular. For landscapes, a folding sketching easel (2) is ideal. This should be simple to erect and adjust to a comfortable height. The practical box easel (3) combines paintbox and easel in one compact unit. The tilt board or table easel (4) with adjustable height and rake, can support a canvas for indoor subjects.

1 The robust studio easel. **2** The sketching easel. Wooden ones warp and swell, metal ones bend and dent. Telescopic ones cease to telescope. Try them before you buy them. **3** The box easel has a palette, drawer for paints, tilting easel and canvas carrier. **4** The table easel.

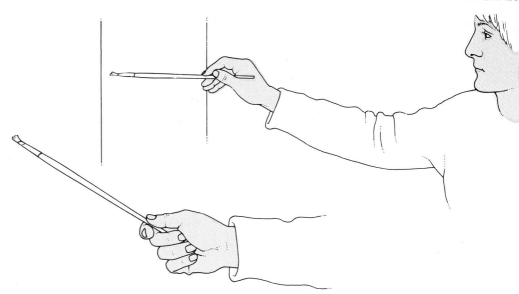

Striking the right attitude

Even if you can't paint well, *look* as though you can! Think of the brush as an extension of yourself. Don't restrict your arm movement and gestures if painting on a large canvas, nor get too close to your work that you stab at it. The movement of the arm from the shoulder, through the elbow and wrist, should be fluid, confident and controlled. Find out just what the brush can do.

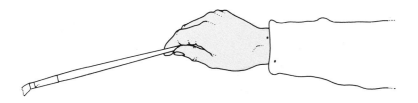

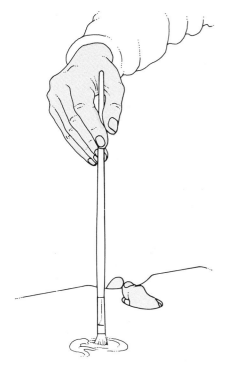

The rhythm of painting

This is not a haphazard thing. Like serving at tennis or changing gears in a car, any rhythm takes a lot of practice. Sometimes, in spite of appearing to do everything right, co-ordination is lacking.

First, look intently at the subject and the canvas, remember what you see, mix the colours on the palette, apply the paint, wipe your brush on the rag over your arm or knee, or rinse it in the white spirit, then look at the subject again. It is important to place yourself so that you are able to see what you are painting as well as the canvas with minimal movement. The memory cannot accurately retain an image for more than a few seconds. If you turn your head away for much longer than this, it is easy to invent what you think you see, rather than interpret it.

How to hold a brush

Hold the brush where it feels naturally balanced but not too near the ferrule. This limits movement to the fingers and encourages brush marks that will be monotonous and restrictive. Put an elastic band or tape around the brush – it will serve as a reminder each time your hand slips down towards the bristles.

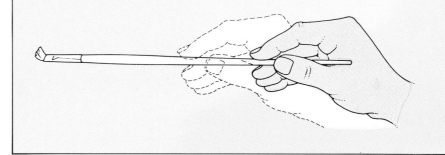

TECHNIQUES

This is perhaps the most important section of the book. It covers all the principles of understanding colour and light, and the actual processes of putting the paint on to the surface of the picture.

Detailed steps take you through all the stages of work, from your initial inspiration and choice of subject, through to planning the picture in terms of composition, bearing in mind the various aspects of colour interaction, line, shape, proportion, harmony and scale, and also the handling of the paint itself.

There are chapters discussing the special factors involved in the main types of subject area. But ultimately painting does not work by any set ''formula'', so the section ends by illustrating some of the broader factors that make for the most original and powerful artistic expression.

These paintings show you several ways to approach one subject, using both brushes and knives to apply the paints, and the different effects you can create. There is no special or "right" way to handle, say, still life or landscape. Any method is acceptable that suits your purpose.

Right: a modern transcription of Titian's *Bacchus and Ariadne,* suggests an abstract approach by focusing on broad shapes, colour and tone.

Left: the objects are fully realized, but the artist's main concern is with the abstract shapes they present.

Below left: a heavier technique is used to create a strong sense of atmosphere, a rich, mellow mood.

Below right: no single figure or object is realistically painted, yet the overall effect gives a perfect impression of a colourful outdoor scene.

BRUSH MARKS

There are no special "marks" to learn for trees, or sky, or water. Any kind of stroke or method of putting on the paint is acceptable. You will feel how the brush responds quite differently on canvas compared to board. Canvas feels springy. Board covered with fabric is solid by comparison. The paint remains on the top and can be built up to look thick and rich.

Each shape of brush is capable of making several marks: you can use only the tip, or press quite hard, or use a dry brush technique. Aim for variety.

Building up with small touches

This style of painting takes time and patience. With a hog filbert start with the darker or middle-toned elements. Each mark, however small, should have a definite shape rather than being purely a mechanical touch. Mix the colours on the palette rather than on the painting or you will end up with a dirty colour. With this method it is not so vital that you build up the picture from dark to light as on such a small scale, the darker colour will sit quite happily on top of the thicker, lighter ones.

Thick paint laid in with a brush

You will soon discover that all pigments have different properties: opaque, translucent, thin or thick. Whites, Naples yellow, the paler earth colours and mixtures containing white tend to be thicker in consistency, darker colours look more luminous if kept thin. Consider early on what elements you wish to emphasize as the thicker areas of paint usually dominate the composition. If you paint a picture in one layer, *alla prima* style (many landscapes are done this way), then keep to simple brush strokes for speed.

Applying thin paint

One of the delights of oil paint is that it has substance, unlike watercolour, which can be manipulated in numerous ways. When paint on a finished picture is too skimpy overall, both this "body" and the glorious richness of the colour is neglected. However, in the initial stages, the general rule is that the larger the area covered the thinner should be the paint. Scrub these in with a large brush. Then you can work progressively from thin to thick, "lean to fat" paint, aiming for variety and balance across the canvas.

Bold, angled strokes

Like handwriting, van Gogh's brush mark has a distinctive style, yet it is much more than just handwriting. Each stroke in his painting (above) was considered and thought out and is charged with controlled energy and liveliness. Cézanne also, in the last ten years of his work, made much use of strokes lying in similar directions so that by means of the angle of the mark he could describe the textured planes of building or the form of a tree. These marks are not for the timid and should be made with a sense of conviction.

Scumbling

The scumble is the result of light opaque paint applied vigorously and fairly dry over previous layers of the painting. It may be stippled, dabbed or dragged over the surface in such a way that the image below can still be discerned, but without definition. The scumble should be allowed to dry before continuing with the work. Scumbling is a drastic way of pulling the tones and colours together. It enables the painter to re-work passages that have become "jumpy" and "out of hand". Unlike glazing, which is sometimes used for the same purpose, it lightens rather than darkens the painting.

Impasto

Often used to give a picture a three-dimensional quality, impasto is thick paint applied generously to the canvas with either a brush or a palette knife. If alternated with thin touches, it gives the surface vitality and variety. Paint and medium (stand oil is good) are mixed together on the palette and applied to the canvas. Shape the paint with the knife. If working with a brush, have it fully loaded, remembering that the marks the brush makes will contribute a dominant textural quality to the painting.

Painting knife

At this stage do not worry too much about how the marks are going down on the canvas but experiment with everything in every way – paint can be scrubbed in rapidly with a brush or painstakingly built up in small touches. The edge of an object can be carefully delineated or large areas of paint laid down with a knife. Choose a knife that is very flexible. The look of the paint will remain fresh and attractive if you put it down decisively, otherwise it could become mannered in appearance.

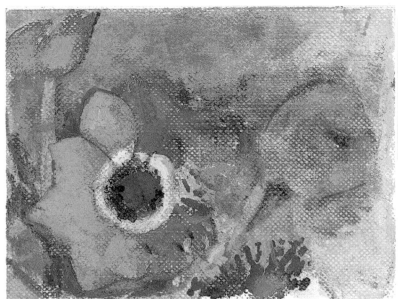

Building up stains

Rather than applying opaque layers of paint, many artists use a palette knife to push the paint into the weave of the canvas, building up a series of blended images composed of translucent stains and resulting in beautiful colours. The paint is applied to the canvas, then scraped down with the knife. As it becomes semi-dry, another layer is added.

Light and dark paint

Dark colours and black should be applied thinly to achieve an effect of depth and richness. Conversely, white and pale colours appear lighter as their thickness and opacity is built up on the canvas.

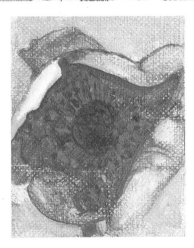

The absorbency of the surface

The texture of the surface and the type of ground you use will affect the marks you make. A non-absorbent ground is needed if you want a rich build-up of paint. If painting in thin layers, or stains, you will need a moderately absorbent ground. The absorption can be varied by altering the proportion of glue size or acrylic to the gesso. More size makes a less absorbent and harder surface; less size gives greater absorbency. Acrylic grounds become more absorbent when diluted with water.

COLOUR WHEEL AND TONAL SCALE

Sunlight is composed of the colours of the spectrum, seen when the different wavelengths of light are split by a prism. The degree to which something absorbs or reflects varying light frequencies if what creates its colouring. The colour wheel is simply the spectrum with its ends joined. Generally colours next to each other produce the purest mixtures, while those opposite make browns and greys. Tone (how light or dark something is) in nature stretches by infinite degrees from bright sun to blackest shadow; you can only generalize this in paint on a very limited scale from white to black.

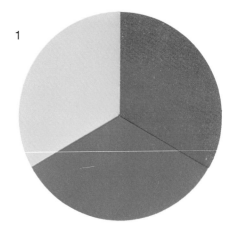

The colour wheel
1 The colours yellow, red and blue are called the primary colours because all other colours can be derived from them.

The tonal scale

It is estimated that if the tones around us are represented on a scale of 1 to 100, pigment can only record about 40 of these. You can try taking a colour (or black) and adding white progressively, keeping the jumps between each tone absolutely even. Establish the mid-tone, then tones between white, mid-tone and black. Now fill in the rest of the scale, aiming for at least 15, adjusting each one to make a smooth series of gradations. Those paintings that take their relative tones from the light end of the scale are said to be in a high key, those from the dark end in a low key. Note the greater tonal variety at the light end of the scale.

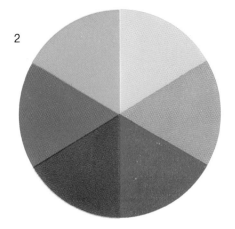

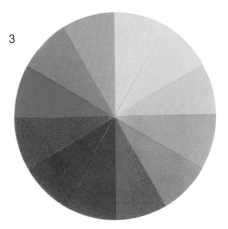

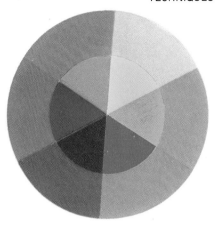

2 Orange, violet and green, because they are derived from the mixture of two primaries, are called the secondary colours.

3 The third wheel shows in more detail some of the intermediate colours occurring as a primary moves through a secondary to another primary, producing tertiary colours, for example blue-greens, pinks and mauves.

Tonal value of colour

The colour wheel of primaries and secondaries shows their equivalent tonal values. Judging the tonal value of things which are themselves coloured requires some practice. Backlighting will lower the tone of an object considerably even if it is light in colour, whereas a darker coloured object in the distance may actually appear lighter in tone than a comparatively pale object in the foreground. This is more apparent when seen through half-closed eyes.

Setting the palette

Painting is about arranging colours to represent something. The range of pigments that come in a tube is so limited compared to the range of colours in life that artists can only make equivalents. The colours of the spectrum are transparent and colours formed by light can never be duplicated by an opaque pigment.

A painting is built on the palette, with each colour separated from but related to its neighbour. A palette should be like an orchestra tuning up – many voices different and distinctive but all with a purpose. There are several systems for laying out colours but you should find one with which you are comfortable and stick to it. You may have already worked out an arrangement you like. Some painters separate the warm colours from the cool colours with a large squeeze of white in the centre at the top, or you could have two blobs of white, one at each end of the other colours. On the palette below, the pigments have been set out in a generally light to dark, warm to cool sequence. A large squeeze of white is placed on the extreme left, working across from yellow to the reds and earths, and at the centre the raw umber that divides the warm and cool colours, finishing with the black on the right. The inclusion of black has often been frowned upon, although every great painter has had it on his palette.

Laying out paints

Put the colours along the top edge of the studio palette so that they do not rub against your clothes, neither too near the edge so that they slide off nor to near the centre so that there is no room for mixing, a process which goes on all the time. A rectangular palette is probably a more practical shape for this purpose.

Selecting your palette

All pigments can now be mixed together. Until recently emerald and the chrome colours were not compatible with black and turned a dirty colour in time. Today almost any colour you need can be mixed from the following range:

Flake white	Ultramarine
Cadmium yellow	Cerulean
Yellow ochre	Viridian
Light red	Ivory black
Cadmium red	Extras:
Alizarin crimson	Raw sienna
Raw umber	Cadmium orange

Pisarro, *View from my window, Eragny.* A sense of cool tranquillity in depicting the landscape elements comes from limiting tonal contrasts, balanced by stronger contrasting colours to represent buildings and figures.

This pair of pictures is an excellent example of the controlled use of colour to create a dominant atmosphere. The squally, wet weather mood is perfectly achieved; note the colour highlights which are used to shape the figures.

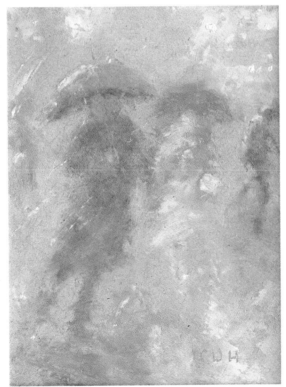

Colour keys

Many colour schemes in paintings are based on colour "keys", that is, a pre-selected basic colour relationship taken from the colour wheel. The simplest system would be a pair of complementaries, red and green for instance, but to avoid harshness and monotony the whole gamut of hues (pure colours), tints (mixed with white) and shades (mixed with black) are brought into play. If this was explained in musical terms, then it would mean that a painting can be composed in a certain key through infinitely subtle variations. This is not the case if you introduce too many different colours into your picture. A large number of opposite colours, instead of making the effect more interesting, in fact end up cancelling each other out. Strong colour contrasts and strong tonal contrasts do not live comfortably side by side on the canvas, although a sharp accent of one colour can be "weighed" effectively against a larger but less intense area of another.

A popular key is the split complementary, greens and orange, blues and red, violets and orange, for example. Sometimes colours from one side of the colour wheel which are harmonious are mainly used, with perhaps small touches from the opposite side, or large areas of greys tinged with colours are offset by pure colours in small quantities.

THE TONAL PAINTING

Tone is the means by which we register the lightness or darkness of a coloured shape as it appears under a particular light. The evaluation of these tonal areas is important in composition, as well as representing the solidity of objects. Study them by making a painting without the added complications of colour. First fix the upper and lower limits of tone, considering each part in relation to all the others as if they were flat shapes, and measuring accurately the lightest plane of the darkest object and darkest plane of the lightest.

Interpreting the tones

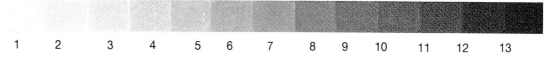

1   2   3   4   5   6   7   8   9   10   11   12   13

Look at your group and try to mix and put down the main tones, from the lightest light to the darkest dark, with only black and white.

1 Plot out your subject fairly simply on paper with pencil or charcoal, defining the main shapes and directions and where the shapes overlap. Then, looking for correspondences and differences in tone, number each area, so that the highlight on the pepper would be 2, the shadow cast by it 7.
2 A half-tone ground on your canvas is a useful guide to help you evaluate the tones. it acts as a middle tone against which to judge the lighter and darker areas. using just ivory black and white lay in the shapes, including the shadows, with thin "turpsy" paint and a medium hog brush.

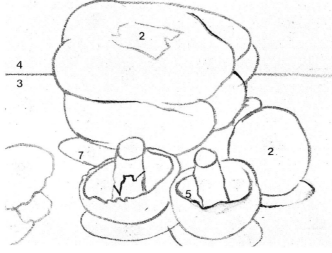

3 With mixtures from only black and white, build up the larger dark masses before the lighter shapes, keeping the tones exact across the picture without any jumps by referring to each shape and your linear drawing, which now bears little resemblance to this final tonal stage.

Seeing tones clearly

Light tones next to dark ones appear lighter than they are. Squinting at the subject with half-closed eyes (far right) cuts out extraneous detail, making it easier to gauge similar values.

Painting in warm and cool colours

Apart from the tonal values of colours, the painter must also distinguish between warm and cool. Most people are familiar with the idea that reds, oranges and browns are warm while the cool colours are grouped at the blue end of the spectrum. However, each colour itself can lean towards warm or cool, you can have a warm blue and a cool green. Neutrals and greys can be either warm or cool depending on what colour is put next to them (see p43). Light varies enormously in temperature according to its source, the seasons or the time of day.

Colour temperatures

Artificial light (warm)

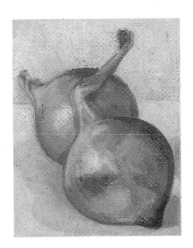

Daylight (cool)

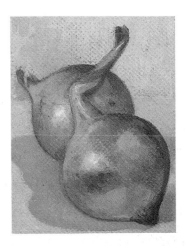

Mixed light (warm/cool)

Sunlight or artificial light accentuates the warm tones of objects, whereas a constant north light may give a cool feeling even to red objects. It is simply a question of looking hard and learning to distinguish the differences. In the first example artificial light creates warm tones; small cool areas appear in the shadows away from the light source. Daylight from a window to the left of the centre group gives a cool silvery quality.

The painting on the right combines both electric light and daylight, which provides a whole variety of warm and cool tones. The cast shadows are not simply a mixture of black and white but contain warm and cool colours which can range from violet to blue. As can be seen in the scale above, when Indian red is added to grey it makes the cool grey progressively warmer. The onions themselves, and the mushrooms opposite, each represent subtle tonal changes.

COLOUR BEHAVIOUR

Practically all the light we see is reflected, and the behaviour of coloured light, when mixed together, is quite unlike paint. Colour is not necessarily bright nor is tone dull. They are modified in appearance by light and shade and by the way they interact: colours adjacent on the wheel tend to be harmonious, complementaries vibrate. The relative weights, warmth or coldness, shapes and their edges all affect behaviour. Concentrate on painting something in the colour you **see** it to be, rather than know it to be.

The definition of colour

Hue means colour at full saturation, that is any pigment straight from the tube unmixed with another colour. Its intensity or saturation describes its strength or weakness. The mixing of white progressively gives a range of colours called tints. Though it is normal to mix white to obtain these tints, black should not be used unthinkingly to darken or subdue colours as muddy 'dead' colours may result. The further apart the colours are on the wheel, the greyer will be the result when they are mixed, so that complementaries will produce subtle and unusual browns and greys.

Saturation

Hue

Although the blue is the same tone

Colour activity

Colours have their own energy and interaction. Look intently at all three squares in the row. In spite of the fact that the blue squares are identical, their colour and tone appear to change in relation to the surrounding sea of colour. Notice how the torn edge of the blue square has more impact than the straight edge. In the second row the same grey square is tinged with green when on the red, looks light on the blue and shifts to darker when against the yellow square.

Advancing and receding colour

It is a common assumption that warm colours advance and cool colours recede. More accurately, more intense colours come forward but so do strong contrasts, impasto and a textured paint surface. In fact, the further any colour recedes from the eye, the more the atmosphere intervenes and cools it off, so that less intense or greyer, cooler colours and close harmonies go back.

in each example, it appears quite different.

The properties of all colours are altered by those adjacent to them.

Colours close in tone enhance one another; strong contrasts lose strength.

TONED GROUNDS

A tinted ground may be less intimidating than pure white for a beginner. Some ground can be left exposed, so choose one which tonally fits your subject, or is a good foil. You could use it as one colour or the middle tone in a sketch where speed is crucial, or cover it entirely; remember it affects all colours you put on top. Adding white pigment to the toning produces a heavy consistency which fills irregularities on coarse canvas or board. Prepare toned grounds at least two weeks before a holiday, so that they dry thoroughly.

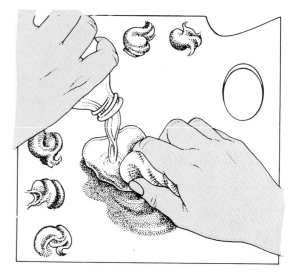

Laying a toned ground

1 At the end of a day's painting the grounds can be mixed from almost any combination of paints left on the palette to tone some other supports. The toning goes over the white primer, whether it be gesso, emulsion or an oil undercoat. Mix the pigments on the palette with white spirit, which dries fast and dries matt. Use a rag to do this.

This landscape illustrates how a toned ground can be used as an integral element in a painting. A pale, greenish ground has been left to show through in several areas.

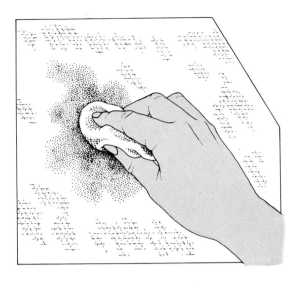

2 Rub the colour on to the primed canvas or panel with a rag, getting it reasonably even. It should look inviting to paint on. Cerulean, ultramarine and raw umber make a useful cool ground, mars violet and raw umber a warm one, and yellow ochre and raw umber a dark ground. Make sure it is thoroughly dry or you will paint it away with the brush.

Underpainting

A toned ground gives an overall colour and sense of unity (sometimes a false one) to a painting. Although the painter does not quite know when the ground is laid how specifically it will affect what goes on top, it can lead to rich glowing colours and to a harmony in the composition, as well as often being left to show through.

Unlike a toned ground, underpainting goes on the canvas in definite areas worked out beforehand and carefully positioned expressly to have an effect on what colour goes over it, to set off another colour and to act as a foil. The increasing transparency of the upper colour allows the lower colour to show through. Giorgio Morandi, the twentieth-century Italian painter whose still lifes are particularly outstanding, used violent reds and greens over which he painted quiet greys. If you were to paint a green apple over red underpaint it would show subtle differences tonally and in colour temperature from a green apple painted over blue.

Some people apply the underpaint using acrylics which dry quickly. Turpentine or white spirit as a medium with the paint also dries fast but later on in the painting you may need to add linseed oil to the medium. You will find that some pigments dry more quickly than others, such as raw umber, cobalt blue and Venetian red, while others take much longer. Mediums such as sun-thickened linseed oil and stand oil are thick and are reputed to enable you to paint on top of a layer of wet underpaint.

How to apply underpaint

Some painters apply underpaint in just one colour, others use several different colours, building up the surface in increasingly "fatter" and more opaque paint. Some simply stain the canvas with a thin wash of colour. As a general rule predominantly cool pictures are painted on warm grounds and warm pictures on cool grounds. (A warm picture on a warm ground could look very "hot".) This is a more considered approach to painting which does not suit everyone's style.

The Renaissance painters achieved their luminous skin tones by underpainting a face in a cool green, thinned down with medium, building up the strong modelling of the cheekbones in a darker tone and the highlights in a pale whisper of colour. When the warm pink flesh tones were slipped over the top they were affected by the shading underneath and appeared coolly beautiful. You can see this for yourself by noticing how the creamy coloured skin of the inside of your wrist makes the red blood in your veins appear to show through as a cool blue, something that both Rubens and Gainsborough had noticed and made full use of in their portraits.

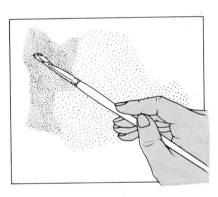

1 Mix paint with turpentine and about 15% oil, making quite a lean mixture. Pour out a little turps at a time, finishing it before putting out more. Lay in the basic shapes or tones.

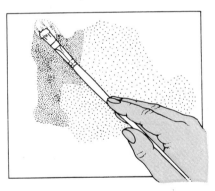

2 How the next layer of paint is affected by the underpaint depends on how it is applied. Often the paint is dragged across the underpaint allow it to show through.

COLOUR OBSERVATION

In nature there is no definition of where one colour starts and finishes. Colour is always on the move, affected by light and shadow, atmosphere, other colours and reflected light from other objects. A seemingly dreary colour may vibrate if set off by another; a warm, glowing colour will alter if an even warmer area is laid down next to it. A painter has to put down *observed* colour, and appreciate that, however subtle, paint can never match the shifting colours of nature.

Choosing a subject

To sharpen your sense of observation set up a few objects, either in closely related colours or perhaps all red or all green objects. Arrange them simply as you will be rendering the subject in abstract form as patches of colour, observing closely the relationships between each one.

Materials you will need

Take a board or canvas and use a brush which will give you one stroke per square of the grid you will construct. See that your still life fits comfortably within the rectangle and is arranged so that a single source of light falls on it.

Mixing colours

Set the palette as usual; colours that are not apparent in the subject may still be needed. It is almost always necessary to mix colours to get what you want. Rarely will two colours from the tube be right without adding another colour or a touch of white.

The colour exercise

Assess and re-mix the colours on the palette until you get them right, never on the canvas. If you want to change a colour already put down, scrape off the wrong colour with a palette knife or wipe it out with a rag. It is usual to overpaint areas in layers and these should be allowed to dry before a correction is made.

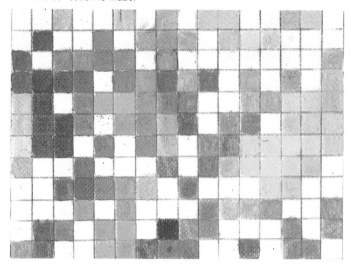

Making the grid

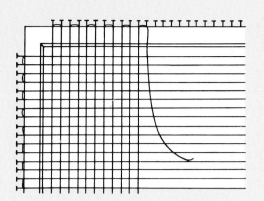

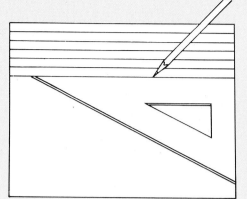

Cut out a cardboard frame, leaving a window about 25 × 30cm. (You could use a picture frame.) Stick in drawing pins at precise 1cm intervals on all four sides. Loop fine grey knitting wool first in one direction and then the other around the pins to form squares. Prop up the grid between your canvas and the subject so that the still life is contained within it.

Now mark off corresponding 1cm divisions along the top and one side of the support. Use a set square to connect up the points. A view from a window can also be treated in the same way by drawing a grid on the glass. or a still life can be set up to reflect in a mirror, the mirror squared up and the grid transferred to the canvas.

First sketch in the main shapes, then start with the most obvious colour or, if in the same colour family, compare and modify each area. Keep the patches in the right place and the right proportions. Colour differences cannot be judged in isolation; they are always relative to each other.

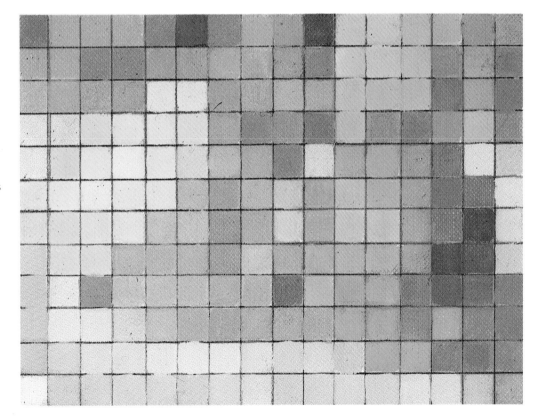

LINE

Pared down to its bare essentials, a painting without the benefit of colour, tone and scale is nothing more than shapes on a two-dimensional surface, connected by lines and directions, imaginary or stated.

Henri Matisse The Pink Nude

What lines do

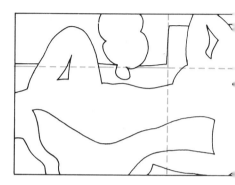

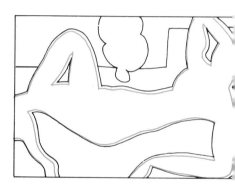

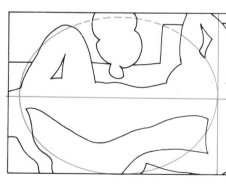

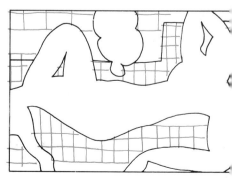

Counterchange

Look for dark elements coming against light ones, which make a foil for light elements coming against dark or middle tones. This induced contrast forms a delightful painterly device.

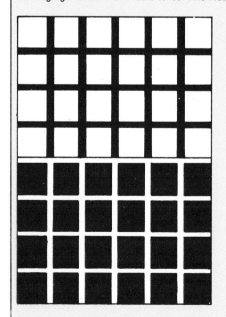

In *The Pink Nude* there are dark squares on light and the reverse.

Here there is a dark shape against light and light against dark.

The qualities of line

Line makes a shape as well as a line. In the painting opposite, the line at the raised knee disappears where the light is probably striking it, while at the calf it is thickened or defined to suggest mass or form. The line can contain the shape within its boundaries, varying in weight (thickness or thinness), in pressure, in tone, in energy, in brightness. It can be washy, dry, soft or hard edged. If you paint a line on top of wet paint, the brush picks it up and this softens the line; if it goes over dry paint, the line tends to look hard. Hogs give a varied line, the shape of which depends on the shape of the brush; the line formed by a sable brush is fine and definite. If the line is the same width all round, the shape of it implies that the picture plane is flat. Although it is easy enough to repeat the same mark – and many painters do – one as seemingly straightforward as line should be put down for a reason and should remain as sensitive and necessary as any other mark you make.

Painting in line

1 Lines divide the rectangle both horizontally and vertically, imply direction and distance, provide an eye level and clarify perspective.

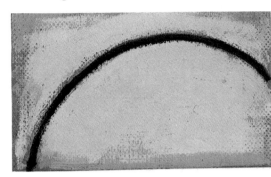

1 Work with the darker line first, painting the light colour up to it, which softens the line.

2 Lines define shapes and give them emphasis, as well as denoting the boundary of a silhouette. They also provide a contrast to the flat areas.

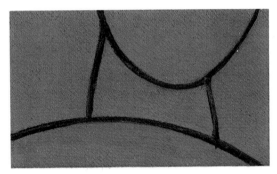

2 Painting a dark line on top of a light colour makes it emphatic, just as leaves painted on top of sky look hard.

3 Lines can be used to create or to build up textures by their colour, weight, repetition or angle, and by the significance of the mark.

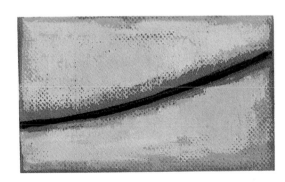

3 In this case the paint is not taken right up to the line. The underpainting is visible to indicate light on the form.

4 Lines establish axes through forms. They can be either straight or curved, not simply horizontal or vertical, and can link up shapes.

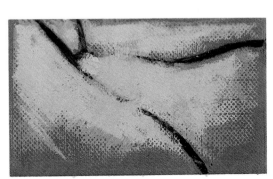

4 Lines have shape and shapes have edges. Painting over the line can give the impression of solidity.

SHAPE AND FORM

The difference between flat shapes and solid form is the way light falls on the object, making one conscious of its solidity. Of course, light and dark is not the only way to represent this; the edge of a silhouette can give the impression of solidity. Light and dark is simply one of the languages of form. For example, if you paint an even edge all round an apple it looks like a cardboard cutout. A contour, however, is affected by the way light falls across the form, obliterating the edge towards the light, defining it on the dark side. The "lost" and "found" painted edges of the outline indicate its volume.

Flat and modulated shapes

Colour in itself is inadequate to describe form. For instance, if you were to take three objects painted in different colours but not illuminated from a particular light source, you could make them look totally flat, that is completely without form. Because of the intervening atmosphere, the further away an object from the eye, the flatter it looks; the closer it is, the more apparent the variation in its colour and in the degree of modulation, which indicates the apple's position in space.

Creating depth on the picture plane

As well as describing solidity and form, shapes also constitute part of the tonal or colour pattern in a picture, while the warmth and coolness of the colours of the shapes and their intensity denote their position in space. You can check this for yourself by cutting a piece of coloured cardboard into three. When each piece is seen at different distances they look dissimilar yet many people would be tempted to paint each one an identical colour, ie their local colour, despite their obvious differences to the naked eye.

The illusion of depth on the picture plane can be generated in two other ways: by the relative scale of the forms themselves, and by the overlapping of the shapes which tells you by the drawing which object is in front of or behind another.

The increase or reduction in size and the directional thrust of the pears suggest depth in the picture. The eye automatically tracks along or extends a line defining shapes and tonal areas.

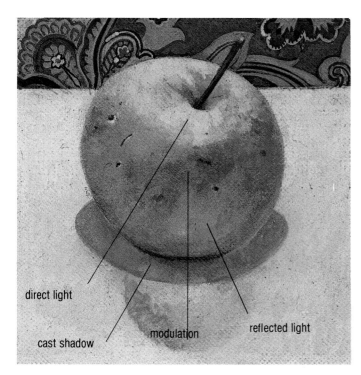

direct light

cast shadow

modulation

reflected light

As a colour modulates, lit by direct or reflected light, it moves through one colour to another across the form. Amateur painters tend to over-model and this can lead to a jumpy or fractured picture surface. Shadows, too, are subject to light and dark, as well as moving between warm and cool, and their subtle colour variations can often be obtained by mixing complementaries.

Representing three dimensions

As it is not possible to actually create three dimensions on a two-dimensional surface, the best you can achieve is an equivalent through the use of tone, colour modulation and the edges of shapes.

In drawing you assume the things in front of you have no colour and to realize their form convincingly you impose on them, by means of shading or the use of light and dark, a system which represents form or mass. This is not true of painting. One cannot assume that everything will look solid by drawing each object with a light side and a dark side. It is the way in which the colour is interpreted on the canvas that creates solidity and planes. Cézanne realized that each plane, turning from the light, became a different colour.

Edges

Flat shapes are represented in three dimensions by the manner in which the edge of the shape is treated. A broken line, a strongly defined one, or simply an indication of where one area of tone ends and another begins, reveals the amount of solidity. Since we have two eyes we actually see two edges to a form. Cover first one eye and then the other and you will see how an object you focus on will move. This facility, which the camera with only a single lens lacks, helps us to recognize that something is round.

Define edges as you go along, building up the paint rather than putting down what you think is there and then re-stating it.

Wall and table are considered at the same time as the fruit. The edge of the lemon is defined away from the light but "lost" where the light falls full on it. The cast shadow modulates from warm to cool in the reflected light of the lemon, one edge sharply delineated or "found", the other edge being fuzzy and soft.

The way in which the shapes of the fruit overlap implies that they are on different planes. Notice the many small changes of colour and how subtly they melt into one another.

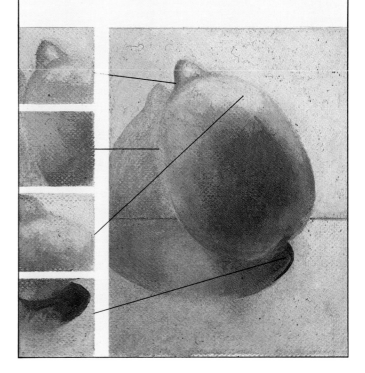

THE BALANCE OF SHAPES

Painting is about the relation of objects, shapes, colours or curves to one another. Fitting the separate parts together in a satisfying way on your canvas is what is meant by composition. Ideally the picture should take its form from the subject itself. Everyone reacts differently to the same landscape, still life or figure. Look for structural devices in other people's paintings and pinpoint what appeals to you – complex shapes played off against something stable, intense colour contrasted with diffuse, definite curves echoed in smaller, less defined curves? Train your eye to recognize various kinds of compositional contrast, without which a painting would be predictable and boring.

Positive and negative shapes

Composition is not just about arranging or defining shapes but, as already mentioned, about balancing or contrasting one area against another. It is a question of creating an equilibrium in the picture so that forces set up within the rectangle are contained, are pleasing to the eye and hold the interest, and combine harmony with variety. If the picture plane were to be divided symmetrically with a centrally placed horizon or tree, for instance, the effect could be dull and boring, and the composition would tend to fall into two halves.

The spaces between the shapes, where it is the leaves on an oak twig or a group of objects in a still life, should be given as much thought as the primary shapes themselves. These "between" shapes should not be treated as background to be filled in later but considered as vital clues to the main shapes, the inter-relationship of the objects and their position in space.

Accurately observed negative shapes can be very helpful to check the accuracy of the positive shapes and establish the form of the composition. Try this experiment. Make a series of drawings of only the negative spaces between the branch of the tree, the leaves and the flowers, filling in these areas in black. You will see that this makes the negative spaces positive. Notice how the spaces between the curves made by the flowers, leaves and twigs are as full of life and energy and as significant to the composition as the plant forms themselves.

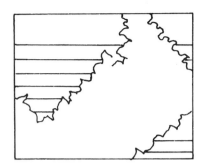

Passive shapes against active shapes

Horizontal and vertical elements in
a painting give symmetry and
stability and can be set off by
active, organic shapes, or by
bisecting the rectangle with a
diagonal force line.

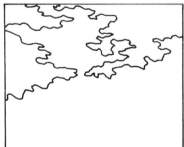

Complex versus simple shapes

Some of the most satisfying
pictures are the simplest. Pin your
tonal drawing to the easel to refer
to when breaking large areas into
more complex ones.

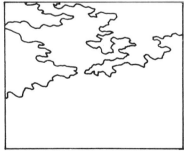

Large shapes contrasted with small shapes

The simple shape of an expanse
of water is played off against the
lively reflections of the lily pads,
the flowers and ripples, delighting
the eye but not dominating the
picture.

FORMAT

The first steps you take in planning a finished work in your mind's eye are vital. The key to this is the composition – having a clearly worked out structure for the image you want to create. But you also must decide on format, choosing a shape for your canvas or board that ties in with your composition plans, and avoids squeezing an idea into an unsuitable shape or area.

1

2

It is not just a matter of convention that some shapes are more suited to some subjects than others. A standard rectangle **1** will allow the eye to move slowly, setting on areas of interest in turn. An elongated shape **2,** on the other hand, encourages free lateral movement.

Squarer shapes **3** are difficult to structure effectively. The elements of the composition need careful positioning. The upright rectangle **4** emphasizes verticals.

3

4

HARMONY AND PROPORTION

There are several methods of dividing up the surface of a painting to achieve a balanced and satisfying whole. One of the most well known, the *Golden Section,* is described below. You will find this is the basis of many famous canvases. For example, *Combing the hair* by Edgar Degas shows a scene of everyday life painted in a free technique, but the harmonious arrangement of the subject corresponds exactly to the Golden Section. But such pictures are also a reminder that these geometric exercises merely create an underlying structure, rather than making effective subjects in themselves.

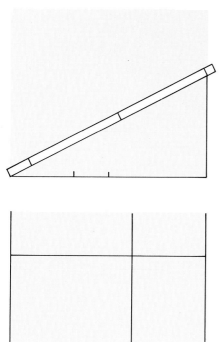

The Golden Section divides a composition particularly effectively. **1** Take a strip of paper and mark the length of the base. Fold it in half to find the mid-point. **2** Mark this distance up the vertical side and take a diagonal to the base corner. **3** Mark the same distance back along the diagonal from the vertical and draw an arc through it to the base. **4** The arc will cut the base at the Golden Section. **5** To find the height of an ideal rectangle from this divided base line, with a square formed by the larger segment, mark the mid-point of the larger segment and draw an arc through the corner of the base furthest from it. Where this crosses the Gold Section vertical will indicate the desired height of the underlying rectangular structure.

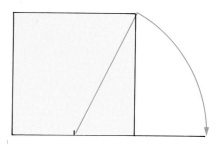

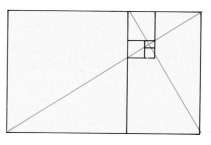

To build a Golden Section from a square, take the mid-point of the base of the square and draw an arc through its top corner (top). Where it crosses the extended base line will mark the edge of a rectangle including a square defined by the Golden Section. From this ideal shape (above), any number of subsidiary Gold Sections can be plotted from the crossing of the diagonals of the whole rectangle and the smaller segment.

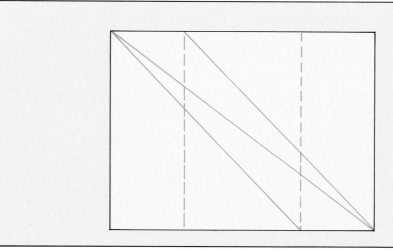

Diagonals
Powerful unifying lines can be found along the various diagonals to be found in a composition. The squares of the rectangle, on either side as shown in the diagram, provide extra diagonals. The zigzag produced by all three can even be used as a device to unite the composition.

Found composition

You can either start a composition as a design which you impose on the shapes and colours of the painting or you can "discover" a pleasing scene that already has the compositional features you want. The latter is the course taken by most outdoor painters, those for whom informality is an important aspect of the work. This does not mean that harmony and proportion can be ignored — they are often the key to the success of the pictures that look least planned. Claude Monet, as an Impressionist, insisted on the validity of unelaborated visual experience, but his *Two Women on the Beach* shows a profound grasp of the principles of composition.

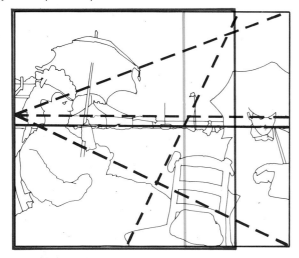

Monet painted the scene very much as he found it, but was also aware of an internal pictorial structure. Always try to find such elements — they will give your work cohesion and balance. In Monet's picture, several factors are involved. First, it is divided into two main parts by the Golden Section (blue). The square of the rectangle (red) forms an independent composition, defined by the vertical made up by

The horizon, placed just above the lateral mid-point, provides a focus for two main diagonals which mirror each other (black). Another diagonal links the top and bottom of the picture. To achieve balance (above), the dark figure to the right is offset by the larger, less heavily shaded woman to the left, the whole effect being a stable but natural composition.

Imposed composition

For some artists, composition is the all important factor, perhaps even the subject of the picture itself. More frequently, an imposed composition is used as a hidden, underlying structure into which the parts of the picture are subtly fitted to create order and balance. This is essentially an intellectual approach to art, and often stems from a preconceived set of aesthetic rules. The criticism, of course, is that such a considered and detached way of planning a painting will reduce the

spontaneity of the artist's creative act, producing dry and mechanical images. While the danger is there, it can easily be overcome. Ruisdael's *Landscape with Ruins,* for example, looks for all the world like an uncomplicated view of a real place, painted from observation. In reality, it owes part of its success to a carefully worked out pictorial structure, with each element controlled by the overall design, although this has not been allowed to dominate the effect of the painting.

The sunlight bursting through the passing clouds gives Ruisdael's picture great freshness and movement. At the same time, the picture is very carefully organized. The church spire, for example, divides the painting exactly on the Golden Section and the horizon does the same laterally (blue). The ruined tower on the right defines the square of the rectangle (red)

precisely. Both these devices create stability. By contrast, the V formed by two diagonals in the foreground (black) leads the eye back into the picture. The artist also created tonal balance through the picture by inserting a light element into the dark foreground with the ruin at the right, corresponding to the dark clouds in the light sky at the top left.

INVESTIGATING YOUR SUBJECT

A still life is an excellent choice to start exploring relationships of colour, tone and shape. As it neither moves or breathes, you can study it at length. The simplest consists of one motif – an apple for instance. Two apples require arrangement – one could sit in the shadow of the other, be cut by the edge of the canvas, or its shadow can form a third shape. Larger groups of objects may appeal because of the pattern they make or their symmetry. Still life also means you can experiment with unusual canvas shapes – long and thin, or tall.

Looking at the subject

When painting from direct observation, the artist has to make two choices: where the viewpoint will be and how much to take in. Both these decisions depend on what has excited you about the scene. A bag of shopping on a kitchen table or tools on a workbench will be on a single level so you might work up close, keeping an eye on the slight distortion of the perspective. From a greater distance you could throw open some cupboard doors and paint the contents ranged on the shelves at various levels. Do not leave out unattractive or difficult objects.

Masking the subject

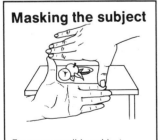

Frame a possible subject, using your fingers or a paper mask. Explore every potential viewpoint.

2

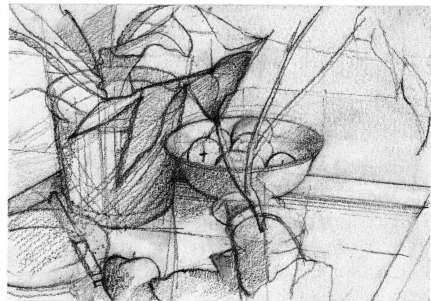

3

Pencil sketches

Pencil drawings teach you to see the picture possibilities in a scene, enabling you to understand the shapes of individual objects and how they relate to one another. This will sharpen your sense of observation – more important than style at this stage. Try to see the broad forms rather than details. Simple line drawings **1** will show how objects relate in outline shape. Additional modelling of the forms **2** will begin to indicate the tonal areas. Even the most simple elements **3** may be sufficient, and moving in close **4** may give a more unusual and interesting view.

4

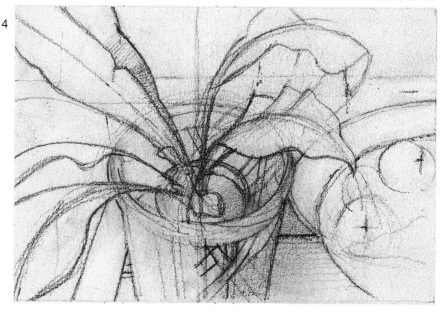

STARTING ON THE CANVAS

Many painters start off with underdrawings, but these may not be elaborate. You can draw straight onto the canvas with a brush, diluting the paint with turpentine. Quick-drying raw umber or ultramarine will work well. Plot the main directions, divisions and axes, referring to the subject or to pencil sketches. Lines dropped from various points establish how the shapes of the composition fall under one another. This method, called plumbing, gives you a rudimentary perspective to work from.

Another method of starting is to underpaint major areas in tones of a neutral colour or a colour close to the one you want. Mix enough of the main colours on the palette to cover all such areas thinly. Keeping to three main tones, apply the thinned paint with a large brush or a rag. To do this you must identify the lightest and darkest tones right at the start. Leave the lightest tonal areas clear and put one touch of paint on each. It is often a good idea to make a tonal drawing rather like a jigsaw puzzle. Refer to this to avoid straying far to the extreme light or dark end of the tonal scale so that small areas of high contrast will have greater effect.

Paint "fat over lean"
For fluid paint with which to cover large areas use only turps with the pigment. This "lean" paint (bottom) dries quickly. With each next layer add linseed oil to the turps — not more than one part to two parts. This is "fat" paint (top). Do not then go back to using turps only.

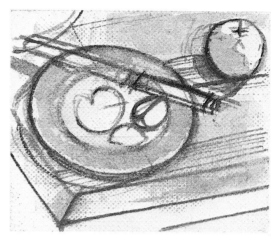

One-off sketch

On a small panel take an initial drawing through to the end in one go. Start with a ground coloured to represent the middle tone. Take care to establish the relationships of tone and colour first time, making sure not to exaggerate the lightest or darkest tones. Spend 30 minutes on this sketch to see how much you can achieve. Mix up the largest area of colour, here the table top. It is most unlikely that pigment straight from the tube will be accurate — other colours will have to be mixed with it. Now try to match the colour of the apple as compared with the colours next to it. Working on several areas of the picture at once you will soon see how strongly colours are affected by those next to them. The colour changes in the apple are more obvious but can you find any in the plate? In your first efforts the edges of the colours will probably meet in a definite line, but you should try to appreciate how colours in life blend into one another.

Shadows are often difficult to paint. The shadows cast by the apple, the plate and the knife are not composed of pigment darkened with grey or black but are colours in their own right. They are also either warm or cool depending on the source of light and on the local colour of the object that is casting them.

LOOKING AT THE COMPOSITION

Always try to see the subject as it really appears, reduced to a pattern of shapes of colour and tone, not as you *expect* it to look. Following the previous pages, you will have now laid down the first exploratory areas of colour, and the tonal divisions between light and dark. As you develop the painting, work over the whole canvas; do not concentrate on detailed passages, as this makes it very difficult to judge how each colour relates to its neighbour. Try to work quite quickly, without rushing, for a controlled sense of urgency will help to keep the picture fresh, a quality which is much harder to maintain if you work over a period of days or weeks. Perishable objects in a still life, such as flowers, fruits or fish, should be worked on more quickly, and it is usually better to develop them in advance of other elements in the arrangement.

A balanced structure

Every painting will have its own tempo, with unforeseen setbacks and even major reworkings occasionally involved. When you have a large part of the surface blocked in, however, you should pause to assess the structure of your work so far. Many of the decisions will have been considered fully at the planning and drawing stage, but at this point new factors must be looked at, such as colour and tonal balance.

Areas of tone and colour and specific shapes can all be said to have values or "weights". Dark areas, for example, have greater weight than light areas. A small area of intense red or blue on one part of the canvas will have greater weight than a larger area of more neutral grey-green elsewhere, even if it is of the same tone. In the same way, shapes with clearly defined edges will weigh more than those with softed edges. It follows that all the dominant shapes and saturated colours should not be grouped on one side of the canvas with amorphous shapes and neutral colours on the other if you want to achieve any sort of balance.

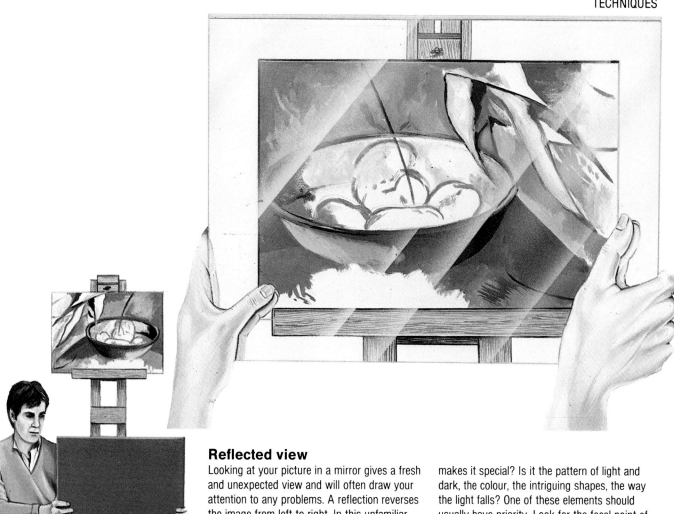

Reflected view

Looking at your picture in a mirror gives a fresh and unexpected view and will often draw your attention to any problems. A reflection reverses the image from left to right. In this unfamiliar form, it may be easier to weigh up the composition objectively. Ask yourself whether what first inspired you is still evident. What makes it special? Is it the pattern of light and dark, the colour, the intriguing shapes, the way the light falls? One of these elements should usually have priority. Look for the focal point of the picture. This can often be where there is the greatest contrast or where the most dominant shapes or colours meet.

Inverted view

Try turning the painting upside down on the easel. Stand right back from it and analyse it. Is there a satisfying arrangement of interlocking areas? Is the eye held in the rectangle or diagonal lines or rhythms lead it out? Is there a main point of interest or do several things compete for attention in the composition?

DEVELOPMENT

A satisfying composition weaves itself into a whole. You can work from large areas to small, or start with the small and build the relationships across the whole, but the important thing is to make constant, careful comparisons of similar colour and tones. Try starting with the area which interests you most. Or you could deal with the parts where objects join up, such as the bowl, background and pot shown below. Repeat touches of colour in different areas.

Work on related areas simultaneously with small touches, fixing the transitions and contrasts across the shapes. Try to find the differences and the connections, to give unity across the whole surface.

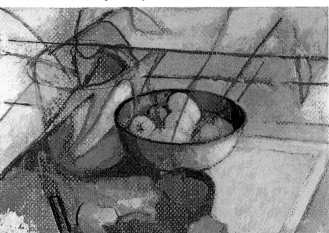

Working from larger areas to small forms

If you feel happier working with larger brushes and generous amounts of paint rather than small touches or marks, concentrate on whole areas, building up from one of them. For instance, establish the background wall, the bowl and the table top before building up the apples or the texture of the plant pot, remembering that you should be working from the translucent darks up to the opaque light colours. When working in small touches, the order in which you apply the paint is not so critical, and any adjustments you want to make can be built up on top of the previous marks. But when making changes in larger areas, scrape the surface of the paint off with a palette knife to prevent the surface becoming sticky and overloaded with paint. Make such alterations freely.

The background should not be treated as a large nondescript area but considered as important as the objects in front of it. Wall and table top should not be left until last nor painted first with the bowl super-imposed on top of them. It is best to build the background areas out from the main areas of interest.

Although a wall may appear to be a flat colour, it is very much affected by the light coming to it. Here, the table top, too, is not a uniform colour but subject to the reflected light and cast shadow of the bowl. Consider the overall colour and tonal relationships.

RESTATING AND ALTERATIONS

Depending on how thickly it is applied, oil paint can take several days to dry. On a wooden panel you will be able to work on it for some time, and even on canvas or board it is possible to make substantial changes if they are required. A picture may, however, lose its freshness with repainting, so try to avoid too much tinkering, but be prepared to make broad changes when you can see what has gone wrong. Work boldly, and remove the sections of paint you feel necessary. Think carefully before alterations, perhaps leaving the picture for a few hours.

"Tonking" with newspaper

When the canvas seems to have become overloaded with paint and still requires further work, the excess paint can be removed by "tonking". Put a sheet of newspaper over the part of the picture that dissatisfies you, rub your hand over it and draw it away. This soaks up excess paint and softens the edges, leaving enough for restatement. The next day, the surface will be dry enough to work on again. This technique results in a dry, powdery surface since much of the oil is absorbed from the paint.

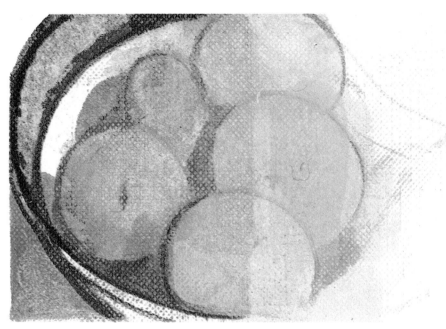

Scraping down with a palette knife

While the paint is still wet it is possible to remove the top layer and alter parts of the composition. Draw the knife across the canvas at an angle to remove the paint from the areas you are not happy with. This takes off more than tonking, but when you come back to the scraped parts of the canvas the image will still remain, although the edges will be lost. Scraping down clears enough paint from the canvas to allow you to see how you might start again, without the distraction or delay involved in overpainting. If painting in small touches, however, overpainting may be easier. Light colours are more opaque and will cover better.

Applying a glaze

Colour can be subtly altered, given luminosity, or a unifying element added, by applying a thin layer of translucent paint over the surface. Transparent or semi-transparent colours usually produce the most effective glazes. Their effect will be to darken the tone slightly. Light areas, such as the highlights on the bowl here, can subsequently be painted over the glaze.

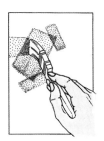

Restating edges

If shapes and colours are incorrect, it is quite possible to redraw them in paint. While you should attempt to position the elements of your composition correctly in the first instance, such reworking is a normal part of oil painting – it is an advantage of the medium.

COMPOSING A STILL LIFE

A still life requires you to both arrange the subjects and to arrange the picture on the canvas. Choose whatever objects appeal from the wide range of possibilities, from pebbles to peapods. Your theme may be a single object or groups; one object dominant in size or colour; a row of varied shapes; an all-over pattern of small items. Work on a 30 × 50cm canvas, choosing a white ground for luminous colours, or a tinted ground for a predominantly tonal group.

Placing objects

First explore various viewpoints on paper. How will you arrange things within the confines of the canvas? Will the group be contained within the space or break out from it?

Be aware of the intervals or negative shapes between objects placed in a row. When objects overlap, look at the subtle gradations from warm to cool in the individual shapes.

Light

Although you can have two different light sources, one artificial and one natural, do not start off with one source of light and switch to another as this will radically alter the warm and cool values. Electric light will give clear, strong shadows and is warm so that colours such as yellow need care. Daylight is cool; shadows will be much more subtle. Shadows can sometimes link single objects that might otherwise be isolated.

Depth and background

Where will the horizon come? Is it to be a shallow or deep group? Will the picture be tall or long? Take it all in in one eyeful, about a 60-degree angle. Remember that you take in more widthways if it is not a very tall group and more in height if the grouping is not too wide. Look beyond

your still life. Is there patterned wallpaper, the handles of a cupboard or the line of a window to include? Consider the play of textures, a surface quality which is a quite separate element from pattern.

PAINTING FLOWERS

Flower painting can be approached in two ways: a botanical style of drawing which is not suited to oil paint, and a more painterly style which makes the most of the richness of oils to suggest the colour and forms of plants. Look carefully for colour variation. A red rose, for example, will be crimson, scarlet, violet pink and peachy pink. Try to capture the freshness and strength of the living organism, rather than copying the delicacy of their precise outlines.

Flower painting composition

- Mass leaf shapes against smaller flowers and do not space them evenly.
- Flowers facing straight on command the most attention. They can be painted with greater definition and emphasis. The other blooms can be given a less dominant role.
- Build the flower heads as a series of portraits each with its own character.
- If the arrangement is lit from one side, the areas facing the light will be more detailed and defined.
- Branches of foliage add graceful curves.

Right: a delightful flower composition by Diana M. Armfield.

Starting to paint

Use the biggest hog filbert brushes you can manage. They will help you to see things in patches of colour. Sables "lick" the paint – and also wear out more quickly. If the ground is not too absorbent you will be able to go on pushing the paint around for some time. An absorbent surface will give a very flat, simple quality. A white ground will produce light, bright colours but may take more time to cover and the flowers could be past their best too soon. A toned ground will help you make quicker progress at the start – a warm ground for cool violet blooms, for example – and will give a rich and luscious effect.

1 With thin paint, establish a firm linear structure of the angles, curves and divisions you decide are important. Look for linking rhythms from one flower to another and between the edges of the shadows.

2 On this scaffolding mass the main shapes and colours of flowers and leaves, scrubbing in thin paint to suggest the whole composition. Indicate with touches on the canvas darkest and lightest tones.

Arranging flowers

If you take flowers from the garden, choose a mixture of sizes, shapes and colours. Arrange them casually in your hand as you pick them, then put them straight into the container you have chosen to paint them in. Place the flowers informally so that they are not spaced too regularly, bearing in mind that you are composing colours and patterns. Cut the stems diagonally, and if possible put some foxglove leaves or a commercial product with the same enlivening property in the water and stand the flowers in it. Put them to one side. The next day they will stay in one position.

3 Now with fatter paint build up the key flower first, painting it as a blend of small shapes of modulating colours and subtle tonal changes. Then paint the one next to it and so on, varying the weight of colour and edges.

4 Instead of concentrating on each flower in turn as in 3, you could work on the whole canvas simultaneously, refining shapes and colours. Work from the dark areas to the light, finally emphasizing one or two flowers.

PAINTING THE FIGURE

Figure painting, especially portraits and nudes, have always been important subjects for artists. In addition to individual studies, figures may form the central element in a narrative picture, or a focal point in a landscape or interior. Figure painting is a special challenge, requiring extra care and preparation. A stylized rather than "realistic" approach is quite acceptable, but remember that distorted figures in many paintings by modern masters, such as Picasso or Modigliani, are like that for a deliberate expressive purpose, not through any lack of skill.

Studying tone and shape

Try to identify the main shapes and tonal areas. Working in pencil or charcoal, pick out the shadows. Mark the darkest area first, working in patches according to the lightly sketched outline. Add the middle tones, and choose the area that will be the most important highlight. This can be left as white paper or emphasized with white conté.

Squaring up

To transfer a small drawing to a larger canvas, divide it up with a grid pattern. This is usually a straightforward grid of vertical and horizontal lines. Transfer the grid to the canvas by laying the drawing on it and extending a diagonal. This will reproduce the proportions. Divide the rectangle into the same number of squares and copy the drawing on the grid.

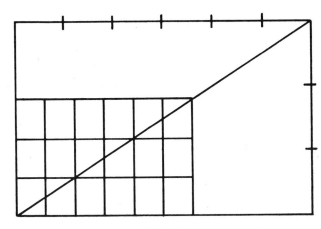

A tonal painting

As a very useful exercise, try painting a picture in light and dark. Work on a ground that serves as a middle tone, adding the dark areas first, as with the tonal drawing. Use thin paint, in broad areas. Pick out the main highlights in a light-toned colour. You should now have the general shapes indicated in position by the areas of light and dark.

Use this simplified image as a basis, refining it but not altering it. Mix four tones of grey on the palette and adjust the neutral ground. Put lighter tones over dark to show the lighter areas. It is easier to paint light over dark than the other way round, but try both. Keep shapes simple and do not include the smaller forms.

COLOUR AND FORM

The main textures encountered in figure painting are flesh, hair, and various types of clothing. Flesh colouring is particularly tricky, and requires the artist to look without any preconceived ideas. Remember it is never, say, a simple, overall pink, but consists of many colours such as reds and blues, and of course the widely different natural skin types present quite different pigmentations and colour tones. You also need to consider the darkening of shadows and the colours of reflected light. Observe these areas of colour and tone, and use them to give the body its rounded forms.

The palette of colours
Rub a new palette with linseed oil to create a good surface. Use a limited range – white, lemon yellow, alizarin crimson and cobalt blue will be all you need. Mix a dark and a light flesh tone with plenty of space to add colour variations to the edges of each.

Clothing in figure painting
Clothes will often occupy more of the canvas than the flesh they reveal. They may have a character of their own which complements and extends the figure subject. First of all, study how they follow the shape of the body – or disguise it. Decide how important you want them to be. They should only be allowed to dominate by conscious intention. Shiny textures, suggested by relatively strong highlights and reflections, or strong patterns, for example, may be distracting. Suggest pattern by the shapes of folded colour you see, rather than laboriously copying the design.

1 Begin with the underlying form and sketch in the broad shapes. As anatomy is to the body, so the body is to clothes. At the same time, ample or loose material may fall into independent volumes. Look for hints of colour in the shadows, such as the blue beneath the hip, and add it at an early stage.

Painting a self-portrait

A self-portrait is a good way to start, giving good practice in painting flesh and hair. For this purpose, worry less about the likeness and concentrate on the tones and colours of the skin. Choosing a composition that closes in on one cheek, for example, might be a good idea.

Setting up a self-portrait

Use a small canvas – as little as 24 × 20cm will do – placed conveniently on the easel. A mirror next to the canvas will provide the image from which you work. Tint the canvas to a light neutral colour by rubbing in thinned down lamp black to give a luminous grey.

Use a warm underpainting, perhaps sepia, to set the form of the head. Add the principal light and dark flesh tones, then the variations of colour you can perceive in the skin.

2 Work over the whole canvas to establish the relationships between the colours of clothing and body. The background is just as important – it too will contribute to the colour effect of the complete work. Distinguish the areas of light, middle and dark clearly. They will underpin and define the painting's underlying structure.

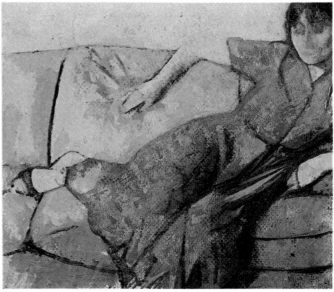

3 To introduce folds and texture, work into the areas of tone you have established. Try not to alter the balance you have set, however. Folds and texture work together. The reflected colours in the shadows and the strength of the highlights will show how dense or shiny is the surface of the material you are painting.

PAINTING PORTRAITS

In theory a portrait is just like any other painting, a question of putting down visual appearances accurately. But because the subject is a person, there are some special factors involved. A physical likeness may prove elusive, and it is easy to get bogged down struggling to make the painting look like the sitter. Concentrate on what you actually see, establishing the general proportional relationships between the features when drawing. Try working from the centre of the face outwards, placing each part in turn. Do not be afraid to make alterations, but draw on top rather than rubbing out. You should also try to grasp the sitter's personality, which may be revealed in body posture and hands as well as the facial expression. Background and other items in the scene can also help you suggest what is special about the person you are painting.

Preliminary drawings
Preliminary drawings are important to help you find the pose that suits your intentions best. Try experimenting with both pose and lighting by making bold drawings with the sitter in a number of positions and with the light coming from different directions. Draw in broad tonal areas – you will learn about the sitter as you go along. Do not expect to achieve a perfect and convincing likeness with your first strokes.

Painting a portrait

You should be prepared to experiment to find what interests you most. In this example, the task is simplified by backlighting. Sketch the general shapes in lightly with brush, marking in some touches of colour for reference. Then try to build up the tonal structure, placing the features carefully but without becoming distracted by the smaller forms. Even when refining the work, remember that too close definition of the features may reduce the likeness and look less lifelike.

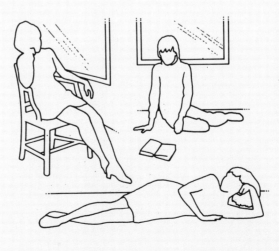

Selecting a pose

Portraits are likely to take a number of sittings and require concentration from both artist and model. Make sure the sitter is in a comfortable sitting, standing or lying pose at the start. Allow the model to move freely when you are not working on face or hands.

Left: note the interesting use of angular shapes and lines in this crisp, clear portrait.

Left and above (detail): in this self-portrait, the use of the fan is a highly effective device, focussing attention dramatically on the single, expressive eye.

Above: this sombre study is an example of highly abstract portraiture, yet the essential forms of the head and face are still traceable.

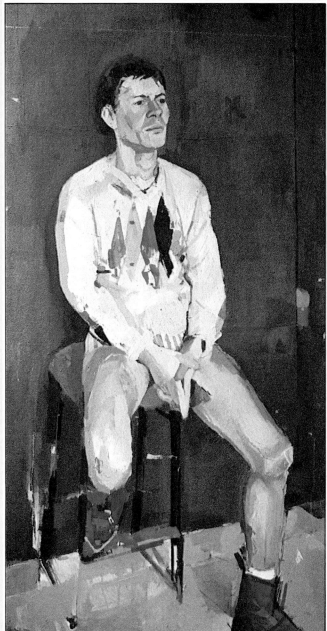

Left: the background and its artefacts play a major role in this powerful portrait, as does the distorted perspective which is used to emphasize the subject's hands.

Above: this aggressively virile study deliberately uses the hands to suggest the sitter's sexuality as a focal point in the portrait.

SCALE AND DISTANCE

In some paintings you may want to place figures or other objects convincingly in space. Conventional representation is not, of course, essential – it is up to you to decide how important you want the illusion of space to be. Many artists have concentrated instead on the picture surface, on the relationships between forms and colours. But here are the techniques that help to set objects in space.

Creating depth

Varying the size of the subject Objects such as figures that are known to be of a similar size will create an illusion of depth if they are painted at different sizes in the same picture. This is a standard perspective effect that can be used quite boldly if you wish to establish several distinct planes in order to lead the eye into the picture.

Aerial perspective Because of the effect of air scattering the different wavelengths of light at different rates, objects at a great distance may appear bluish grey. Objects in the middle distance appear more muted in colour than those in the foreground. Again, separate planes can be established in the picture in this way.

Linear perspective As objects appear smaller with distance, parallel lines that recede into a scene will appear to come together. By including lines of objects in the composition that converge towards a "vanishing point" on the horizon, a great impression of distance and space can be simply created.

Placing the subject within the picture area can radically affect its importance relative to the other elements in the painting. The centre foreground is usually the dominant place. Moving the subject further up the picture also may create an impression that it is further away – even if it is in fact painted to the same size on the canvas.

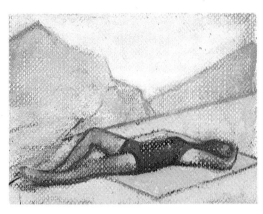

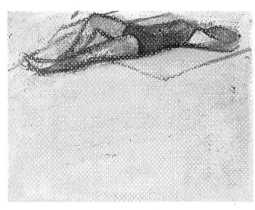

Separate planes Another aid to placing elements satisfactorily in space is to see them as planes, constructing the composition with clearly defined groupings.

Overlapping Objects, including figures, placed in front of or behind each other will suggest depth in the picture. Such arrangements can also unify the composition.

Establishing scale

It is very difficult to judge the intended scale of objects in a picture except by association. Some recognizable shapes are immediately familiar – figures, buildings, animals, for example – and can be used to set not only their own size but also that of other elements placed close to them. Some trees, for instance, could be almost any size, but with a person or a farm animal nearby, it immediately becomes clear whether the tree is large or small. In the same way, if you want to stress the large size of something, place a diminutive figure or building next to it.

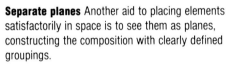

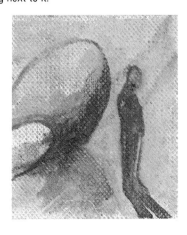

This vague shape is obviously intended to represent a rock, but it is difficult to estimate its scale.

Small on the canvas and placed in relation to a large figure, it is clearly no more than a small boulder.

Towering over a full-length figure, it has much greater impact, becoming a major part of the composition.

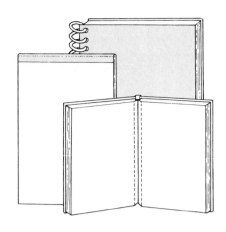

THE SKETCHBOOK

Sketchbook drawings help you to make discoveries about the subject you plan to paint, and may also be intended as detailed working drawings. They should have detailed colour and tonal notes to refer to later at home; these are very useful once you have covered over the initial drawing on the canvas. Do not hurry over the sketchbook stage. While exploring your subject you will be absorbing a great deal of information. Photographs do not help you to learn much about what you mean to paint, or retain your initial inspiration, so use them only as a limited source of information in conjunction with your sketchbook.

Choosing a sketchbook

The word "sketchbook" implies something sketchy, but it is said that if four or five marks are meaningful, they can be more value to a painter than his finished work. A pocket-sized, hard-back, drawing book should have ample pages so that you will not be tempted to be mean with them and be sturdy enough to support the paper as you are drawing. Some have perforated pages and lie flat. Spiral bound books, although they stay open, tend to rub the pencil marks.

Sketching outside

When you arrive at the spot where you would like to paint, a lot of time can be wasted looking for the ideal view. Sit down and get to work, investigating the various possibilities in numerous pencil sketches. Then single out one or two viewpoints that particularly appeal to you and do a really thorough drawing of the composition. Ask yourself what features it has that attract you and draw small studies of these as well. Include as much detail as you will need for completing the painting at home, and make sure the drawings do give you that information. You may be intrigued by the interplay of different shapes, the silhouettes of trees and buildings or by the tonal contrasts.

Tonal range in a landscape

Tones are particularly important to note and you should check that these remain consistent across the canvas. Notice right at the beginning where the tonal scale falls – is the picture in a high of low key or are the tones all in the middle range? In a landscape there is usually nothing very white or very black. In direct sunlight, shadows may be deep, but they are unlikely to be as dark as they first appear. Light is usually diffused by haze or cloud, although storms are exceptional, giving strong contrast.

The eye is attracted by the lightest thing in a picture or the place of most contrast. Keep the lightest area small and within the rectangle, not drifting off to the edge. The real darks should also be small. Be aware of the similarities and contrasts between tonal areas and the richness and variety to be achieved by the arrangement of these light, dark and middle tones.

Many different, and often ingenious, methods have been evolved to make notations of colour and tone in a landscape. Some artists cover their drawings with written notes, although you may find that words on a small drawing can sometimes confuse the tones. Other painters make a dot in the centre of the area of colour, then draw a swift line from it to the outside edge where they make their notes. Some use series of dots which act as reminders. You will have to feel your way until you have a system that works for you and becomes a personal shorthand, a code that trips your memory of the scene. However, it will be of no use at all if you are not able to read it back.

Making pen and wash drawings

Tone can be suggested with pencil as below or with ink. Using a pen alone, shadows have to be built up with hatching, giving a precise result.

A more free and subtle sketch can be made with washes over the ink outline. Keep the washes to a minimum and match the tones you see.

On top of the wash drawing, the pen can be used again to pick out the deeper shadows. If the wash is wet, these darks will run and look softer.

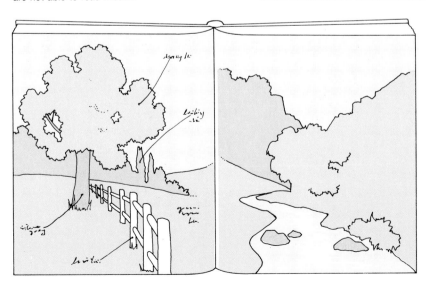

You can record colour as written notes by association – for instance, noting that an area of sky is "pearly grey" or "lemon yellow" or that it matches the colour of your blue sweater. Or you might prefer to write down the actual names of the pigments, such as "burnt sienna with a touch of ultramarine." Try to be as accurate as you can.

Another method is to use a numbering system that denotes the relative values of the colours. Thus, B1 (blue 1) would represent the brightest blue and B5 would signify just a hint of blue. You should also indicate on your drawing the modulation of the colours in the scene. Changing colours could be noted with an arrow.

PAINTING LANDSCAPES

A primed toned board or coloured cardboard may be more practical and less easily damaged outdoors than canvas. You can start and finish anywhere on a panel, and trim or centre later. Oil painting paper can be tacked to board. Hog filberts in sizes 4, 5 and 6 will cover the canvas quickly. Don't skimp on your valuable drawing time. Nothing in landscape stands still, and the time of day and weather will dictate the speed you need to work.

Working to a time limit

Ask yourself, how much time do I have and what can I achieve in that time? As the weather and the light are altering every few minutes, you have two choices: either to capture a fleeting impression in an oil sketch, or to start something on the spot, perhaps to be completed at home.

During the early morning and evening hours the scene will change rapidly – within an hour four or five different compositions may pass in front of your canvas. In the middle of the day things will not vary as much and you will be able to spend more time on one canvas. You should reckon on having about 15 minutes close to dawn, 30 minutes in the early morning, two hours at midday and about 15 minutes again in the evening. Early or late in the day, decrease the size of the canvas. In the middle of the day the size can grow. As soon as the view changes, change the canvas rather than the composition, and go on with the first picture next day.

Selecting the subject

Frame up the view with your hands or use a rectangular cardboard window. Think about scale: do not try to cram a panorama onto a small panel or fill a large canvas with a small motif or too many tiny forms.

If you take in an angle of view of more than 60 degrees you will have to scan, and then cannot judge perspective accurately. A narrower view will quite often strengthen the composition by emphasizing the individuality of each shape. For example, if there are 20 trees in your wide view, they will not only look similar but appear so in the picture. Pick out two or three and suddenly there will be a much sharper contrast in their shapes, scales and detail.

Response to the subject matter

What is it that affects you about this particular bit of the landscape? Is it to be a painting where the eye "reads" or moves across the canvas in an anecdotal way, or one with a strong focal point?

Start by isolating the area you are going to paint and thinking about the proportion and scale of it. Select a piece of board or a canvas suitable for the shape of that idea. Pin the relevant drawings up on your easel or painting-box lid to remind yourself of the wide scope of your chosen subject because, as your tempo changes from excited response to serious, organized painting, you may lose the feel for the whole composition. Finally, lay out your palette in the normal way.

How to start

Speed is important in the field and here a toned ground has its advantages. Almost any colour will tone the ground or use a general colour from the composition and apply it with a rag, a housepainting brush or a large hog. The paint should be thinned down with turpentine or white spirit to cover the whole canvas. This will dry quickly. Or, without any added thinner, lay the underpaint over the canvas, scrubbing it in with a vigorous brush movement or a rag. Once that is done, you can develop the scene in a linear way, or concentrate on larger areas. In a one-off painting there is usually no time for over-painting in layers and thick "fat" paint can soon get into a sticky mess, so you will have to scrape down or tonk (see p66).

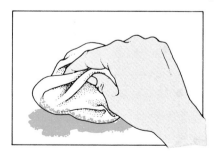

A dark, glowing stain can be achieved by applying thick paint and rubbing it off with a rag, and is more powerful than brushing on thinned paint.

Laying in thick paint with a palette knife straight onto the primed canvas covers the surface quickly and is good for covering large areas.

Quick oil sketches

With quick sketches, do not try to take in too much. Work to a small scale – a small board such as 15 × 20cm will be sufficient. Even with a more elaborate two-hour sketch, limit the size to 50 × 60cm. In this case, work in the middle of the day, when the light changes will be slower.

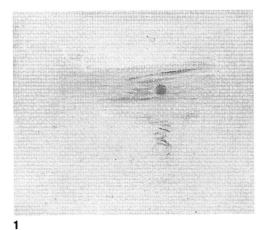

1

2

15-minute sketch

1 Use the rapid sketch as a means of recording a first impression and opening up your technique with oil paint. Try using a rag, cotton wool buds or your finger, working in one layer.

2 As you develop the sketch, do not be distracted from the aspects of the scene that first attracted you. If your ideas change about the approach to the subject, put up a new canvas and start afresh.

Two-hour sketch

With a more finished sketch, relatively complex compositions can be taken on. Following the approach taken here: **1** Identify and set down the most prominent areas of pure colour as a series of small touches. **2** Then add the other tones, relating them to the keys you have already established. **3** If the original idea becomes lost as you work, scrape down the thick paint, leaving only the impression of the colours. **4** The final sketch can then be built up from this base.

1

2

3

4

Colour in landscape

Look at the most obvious colours in a landscape, green and blue, and compare them. How blue is the sky? How green is the hedge? How yellow is the meadow? These local colours must be made to fit into the tonal scheme of the whole picture. Green is a particularly dangerous colour, and landscapes are often saturated with it. It is possibly the most difficult colour to use over large areas and needs to be tempered with other colours as well as contrasting warm and cool greens to keep them lively and singing. Your paintings will be much more convincing if you avoid the art shops' "sap greens" and "grass greens" and mix your own from lemon yellow, yellow ochre, cobalt and ultramarine, where necessary adding some red or possibly a bit of black. If you do not attempt to do this you will find yourself using the same green everywhere and the end result will be dull and unrealistic.

Green: the colour range

Green fields in the foreground become increasingly blue in the distance because of the effects of aerial perspective (p80). As a result, you can expect to see the strongest greens in the foreground. What you think should be a green tree on a distant hill may not be green at all in comparison to the field at your feet, but brown or grey or blue. Look at the green label on the paint tube or the blob of paint on the palette and ask yourself: Is that field really the same green?

Building the picture

A complex landscape worked on over several sessions is more dependent on a firm structure of shapes, rhythms and tones than on capturing the transitory moment. First, you should keep a constant watch on the original drawing. The eye is often pulled to the lightest spot, the brightest colour or where there is an area of most contrast or activity. Make sure that their importance or emphasis has not been lost. Second, find a key point in your composition to refer back to. This will keep your drawing and painting accurate and true to your first idea. Third do not be afraid to restate or redraw as you progress. After a day's painting take your work home and scrape it down if it is sticky, put it up where you can see it and study it carefully. Sometimes it is helpful to turn it around and leave it for a week. Later, you can often see where it has gone wrong and will be able to work on it with a fresh approach.

Finishing touches

With the major areas of colour and tone laid down, decide how much finish you intend the picture to have. it is easy to spoil your work by labouring over details. Instead, look for the highlights, even a tiny speck of light as the sun catches the underside of a leaf. You may also want to deepen some shadows to enhance the tonal range.

Tree forms

Do not dismiss trees with a vague outline, nor paint every leaf. Individual leaves cannot be seen except at edges or in close-up. See trees as a sculpture of solid forms, and note the proportions of the trunk.

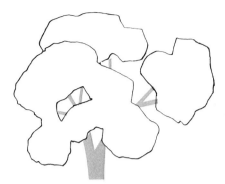

Trees and foliage

Trees should be painted as vital, living things rather than masses of limp cotton wool. In winter they form powerful shapes. If you paint a dark tree on top of a light sky, are you simply following a preconceived notion of a tree? If you paint the tree first and then the sky up against it, you will be conscious of the negative shapes around the form, in fact you will redraw the tree and really observe it much more intently. Consider the branches and the tree's distinguishing shape. Where the sky is visible through a tree in full leaf it should be treated with great care – these shapes make the tree look realistic. Detailed drawings of leaves, branches and bark are useful for later reference. Wood is not a uniform brown but ranges from grey-green to pinky brown. Its colour needs special care – it is impossible to show it convincingly with brown pigment straight from the tube.

Painting trees

In summer, groups of leafy trees, as well as grasses and bushes or individual clumps of leaves, can be defined on the canvas as masses divided into dark and light by the sunlight. Do not paint the visible branches evenly silhouetted. Choose one and follow it to the tip of the branch, making sure that it neither looks lifeless nor scratchy.

Skies and clouds

Light and colour in a landscape are a direct reflection of what is going on in the sky. Some skies have pink, yellow, green and violet tones, besides white, grey and blue. Colour varies from the top to the bottom of the sky, and differs from left to right depending on where the sun is. Clouds are rarely pure white; Naples yellow is often useful for warmer areas. They are constantly changing, ethereal shapes, so aim to capture their colours correctly, rather than any accurate shaping.

Painting sky and clouds

Clouds should not be left to the end but worked on as an integral part of the picture. Identify the broad shapes and try to relate these to the lower part of the picture to add compositional unity to the landscape.

Different approaches to landscape and seascape. **Left:** a crisply realistic photographic quality is displayed here. **Below left:** a riot of colour, boldly applied, creates a marvellous atmosphere of Mediterranean warmth. **Right:** a further degree of abstraction, with the main interest in the strong blocks of colour which are used to create a sense of place.
Below right: the artist has chosen a limited, mundane view to successfully establish a particular atmosphere in this beach scene.

SEASCAPE

The sea offers a superb subject for paintings. The sense it gives of the vast scale of nature and the drama of its moods are a wonderful source of inspiration. The shore is the best place to find suitable views, with the sea meeting the land in high cliffs, sweeping beaches or windswept dunes. Although the sea can be violent, the broad horizon and even expanses of water and sky more often have a soothing effect, and the subject matter can be interpreted in many ways, even as abstract patterns.

Painting a seascape

1 Spend some time selecting a view and sketching; then choose a canvas. Start with the basic division of the horizon — sea against sky. First decide where your greatest interest lies. Is it in the water, the sky, or the colour and activity on the beach? Sometimes it is not in the foreground at all but on the horizon. Now rub in the main tonal areas.

Water: ripples and reflections

Study the rhythm of ripples. Although widely spaced in the foreground, they close up in the distance. See how the larger patterns make smaller shapes, rounded to suggest liquid form.

Where land and sea meet is often the point of most activity. As the tides rise and fall, there may be overlapping ripples on the shore, tidal pools, breakers crashing against the rocks, or simply a change from light to dark.

Reflections can be bright or subtle patterns of colour — an upside-down view of the scene.

2 The sea is like a fragmented mirror reflecting all that is going on in the sky and so it must bear some relation to it. As it is a vast area that changes all the time, you must be prepared to paint quickly. Build up broad areas over the water, the sky and the land, relating colours across the canvas and establishing the tonal range.

3 The colour and brightness of the water depends on its clarity – river water seldom has the same sparkle as the sea – and on the quality of the light. Here the white ground gives a high-key luminosity. Look out for the marvellous contrast between the local colour of the tiled roofs, boats, deckchairs and swimsuits and the subtle colours of nature.

Drawn and painted studies

Boats consist of a series of curves which are difficult to paint. One way to overcome this is to build them up by referring to the shapes on either side of them. Think beyond trying to portray the actual structure of boats. They will be more convincing if painted simply in terms of shape, colour and curves to create pattern.

Salt water and sea shore are a rich source of study material, from shells to marine plants. If you cannot get to the coast, you could visit a local fishmonger or aquarium.

TOWNS AND BUILDINGS

The sketchbook really comes into its own with townscapes. It is quite possible to work direct, sitting in a street or a café, paintbox on knee, but here you will encounter one of the drawbacks. Who has not, at some time or another, peered over an artist's shoulder? Being the centre of such interest can be very distracting. One answer is to make detailed drawings with full notes surreptitiously behind a newspaper or in a small sketchbook, and complete the painting later in relative privacy.

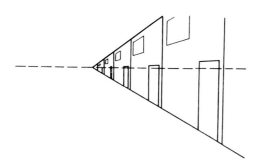

Eye level and scale
Eye level simply means the line which is the same height above the ground as your eye. The horizon, when you can see it, is always on your eye level. If you take a building and draw lines from top and base to meet at the horizon, the relative scale of other buildings can be judged.

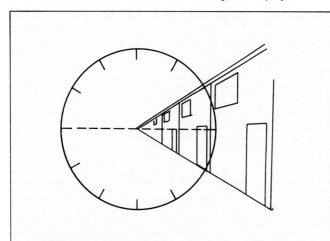

Judging angles
Whether they are above or below you, the top and bottom of any flat vertical surface, such as a building, remain horizontal so long as they are exactly opposite you. When a building is turned from you it becomes subject to perspective. To judge its angles, imagine a clock face centred on the intersection of the angle. You can "read" it, as you would the time.

Buildings
Depending on the style in which you paint, you can include as much or as little architectural detail as you want. In any case, look for the essential shapes of the buildings, putting down their solid forms before moving to incidental details of windows and doors. identifying and plotting in the main vertical right down the canvas, whether it goes that far or not, helps you to see how things fall under one another. In a hot climate, note the direction of the sun and place yourself so that it is at your back for as long as possible, or so that you are in the shade. Shadows are important to the composition as well. Diagonal ones can divide the space, link up shapes and allow you to introduce changes of tone from light to dark. You will be unwise to tackle over-elaborate compositions. Look instead for bold and interesting shapes.

Figures in space

If you stand up or sit down, the eye level in the scene goes up and down too. If you are standing, the heads of figures far or near will all be on a level with your eye and also with the horizon. If you sit and they remain standing, your eye level will be at their waist levels, which will appear to remain constant.

Street signs and other lettering

Whether letters are painted clearly or only hinted at depends on the type of painting, but they can provide a good focus of interest. Look at lettering as shapes rather than words, painting them from the bottom to the top in an attempt to suppress your own calligraphic style.

Reflections in glass and water

A reflection in a window can be gradually painted from the inside to the outside edge. Shadows will obscure parts of the image. A car can be seen as a box of reflections in which you can see yourself, a person walking past, another car or the house across the street.

Reflections in the rain will be less well defined. Colours may be restricted to greys and browns, making the vivid colours of umbrellas and clothing stand out. These provide attractive shapes and silhouettes, both in full view and reflected from the wet streets.

Starting to paint

First of all, choose a vertical or horizontal format. The latter is more suited to broad views including a distant horizon, the former to pictures at street level with the buildings leading the eye up and down. The foreground is important in townscapes — try to use the incidents which naturally occur there in your composition, and do not let the background dominate.

First identify the main blocks made up by the buildings and construct a framework of directional lines to define the main perspective. Here, the buildings follow the rise of a hill, so the point at which the main perspective lines converge is above the horizon.

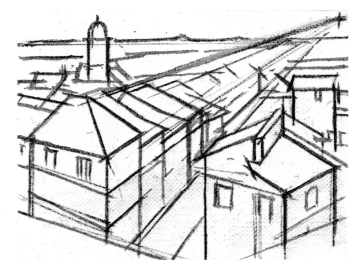

Townscapes ancient and modern. **Below:** a modern, industrialized, urban panorama is presented in considerable detail, and is transformed into an intricate and satisfying pattern of multiple shapes.
Below right: Corot's *Island of San Bartolomeo* is a beautiful example of the harmonious use of colour. Each city or town will tend to have its own characteristic colours, depending on the local building materials and climate.

Building tone into the painting

Having plotted in your linear drawing, or simply indicated a few verticals and the eye level, brush or rub in the main areas of tone in "lean" paint. White spirit dries faster then genuine turps. Mass in the shapes without hard edges at this stage. Define light and dark planes before adding detail.

In warm weather, thin tonal lay-in will take about an hour or so to dry. If in a hurry, you can work directly on to the wet paint, but, when one area of paint has to be put down beside another colour that is still wet, it is likely that they will mix together and look muddy. If light paint goes into a dark area by mistake, it can be covered over quite easily. It is a little more difficult in reverse. The following day, however, the first layer of paint will be dry and you can build on top with "fat" paint.

PAINTING ANIMALS

Animals and birds make excellent subjects for painting, with the variety of their actions and activities, full of different types of dynamism, energy and life. The colours and textures of fur, feathers, skin and scales are an exciting challenge, and in close-up an animal's face can also offer a lot of "character" to be captured. Their shapes also tend to be more simple than the human form, encouraging strong compositions and boldly executed paintings.

Preliminary sketches
Domestic animals Thorough sketching is the key to painting an animal successfully. Pets are good to start on. They make good models as their movements are predictable, allowing regular occasions for study. These preliminary sketches were done in pastel pencil.

Wild animals cause greater problems. It is just as necessary to understand their movements fully, but the opportunities for close study are few. Zoos offer one approach, but while some zoo animals behave naturally, others seem lethargic and depressed. In some cases, you can work in the field, making rapid sketches with the aid of binoculars. You may also consider using photographs as reference. Always make a thorough study of several photographs to gain a full understanding rather than copying from one source.

Composition, shape and texture

It is tempting to take a literal approach when painting animals. Their behaviour is so immediately appealing that just producing a coloured representation may seem a sufficient goal. It is important, however, to remember important compositional elements – even for a straightforward animal portrait. Think, for example, of the areas of canvas that the subject animals will not occupy. In other words, consider the negative shapes around the subject. With a successful pictorial structure, the elements of the composition will fall into place. Textures may also have a major role. Look carefully to see how the light is absorbed by and reflects off the unfamiliar surfaces of fur and feathers. Shiny coats will reflect many interesting colours. Ignore your preconceptions – an elephant, for example, is more likely to be brown than grey – and concentrate on what you actually see.

Animals in a landscape

1 It is unlikely that you will be able to paint wild animals as you watch them, so work from drawings. Concentrate on relating the animals to their environment in a natural way. Outline the main elements of the landscape first and then add the animals as the main focus of interest, perhaps dominating the foreground and ideally forming an integral part of the composition.

2 Work on both animals and landscape at the same time to ensure the unity of the composition. Build up the main areas of colour and tone with thin washes of paint to start with, defining the shapes of the animals and also the negative shapes of the landscape around them. Broadly establish the colour and tonal range of the scene.

Textures of fur, feathers and scales

Fur can be imitated with a hatching of lines painted with a dry brush. Dry paint on top will suggest a downy quality.

A loose working of light into dark and dark into light can build up an effect of short, thick hair over a complex surface.

For long, smooth hair, define more generous areas of colour and tone, with occasional lines to suggest the rhythms of its fall.

3 The swans in this painting pose some interesting problems in handling colour and light. They will not appear as uniformly white as expected and the reflected colours in the shadow areas will include rich blues and violets. Be prepared to simplify the shadows and highlights to build up an effective modelling of the three-dimensional shapes before you.

4 As the focal point of the picture, the swans should receive more attention, with the highlights strongly accented. The other main area of interest is the bank of reeds behind them. Finally, adjust the main lights and darks to unify the lighting and atmosphere of the scene, ensuring that the birds are lit in the same way as the landscape.

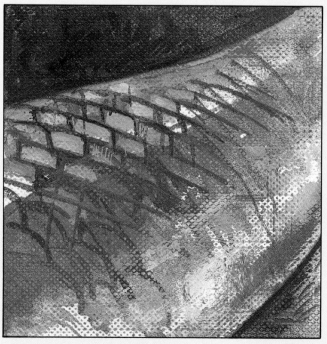

Individual feathers are rarely visible except for the large flight feathers on wings. identify the main areas of light and shadow, and use loose dabbings of dry paint to suggest a downy texture.

The scales of fish and reptiles require you to define the general rounding of the forms more positively. Suggest only a few individual scales and show reflections and sharp highlights.

COLOUR AND EXPRESSION

Colour begins with your palette. Using a limited number of colours will contain the range of hues within the painting; at other times you may want a wide range of pure colours for a more varied chromatic effect. No one can fully explain the response to different colours, but they seem to have direct effects on mood, and arouse very different emotional responses. It is difficult to be precise about this, and responses will certainly vary according to a person's background and upbringing, but some well known examples easily illustrate the point. Think how the strong, vibrant colours of Titian communicate an intense joy in the splendour of the world, or how the shift from Picasso's "Blue" to "Rose" period reflected a change from melancholy to romance and nostalgia.

Classical palette

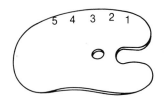

1 lamp black, **6** flake white, **3** yellow ochre, **4** venetian red, **5** terra verte. This palette, consisting of earth colours, offers great tonal range and a satisfyingly restrained harmony. Try using it for a small still life.

Cool palette

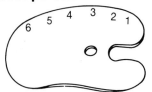

1 titanium white, **2** cerulean blue, **3** cobalt blue, **4** ultramarine, **5** (cadmium yellow), **6** (cadmium red). Here, the effect will be cool, but with two warm colours added (**5** and **6**) an enormous range is possible.

Warm palette

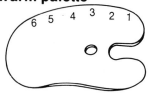

1 titanium white, **2** yellow ochre, **3** cadmium yellow, **4** raw sienna, **5** cadmium red, **6** (cobalt blue). This wam palette is ideal for sunny landscapes.

Warm to cool palette

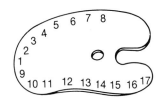

This palette runs from light to dark in two directions: warm and cool. It includes a full range of colours, and sections of the scene can be identified as lying within the warm or the cool range. **1** flake white. Warm: **2** Naples yellow, **3** yellow ochre, **4** cadmium yellow, **5** raw sienna, **6** chrome orange, **7** scarlet lake, **8** burnt umber Cool: **9** lemon yellow, **10** emerald green, **11** viridian, **12** alizarin crimson, **13** cobalt blue, **14** ultramarine, **15** cobalt violet, **16** raw umber, **17** lamp black.

Chromatic palette

Here, for a rich and vivid effect, "synthetic" colours are used to the exclusion of the earth colours. The effect is of the pure colours of light rather than the muted hues of nature.

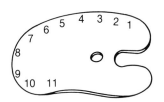

1 titanium white, **2** lemon yellow, **3** cadmium yellow deep, **4** chrome orange, **5** vermilion, **6** cadmium red, **7** alizarin crimson, **8** ultramarine, **9** cerulean blue, **10** cobalt blue, **11** cobalt violet.

Colour	Association	Emotional response
Black and white	Light and dark, good and evil.	Pure whites and blacks are cold and uninviting. Greys can be restful.
Red and orange	Fire, sunsets, danger signs.	Excitement and intense activity. Red is nature's warming colour.
Yellow	Fire, sunshine, flowers.	Provocative and energetic, yellows are cheerful and stimulating.
Earth colours: browns, ochres	The soil, rock, wood and bark.	Warmth and cheer. Invigorating if strong, soothing if lightened.
Green	Growing plants, natural landscape.	Peace and simplicity. Freshness and growth. Nostalgic when mellow.
Blue	Sky, water, space.	Deep blues suggest mystery. Paler blue becomes cold and melancholic.
Violet	Rich velvets, splendour.	Sense of dignity and deep calm. Can be threatening.
Pinks	Rich cloths, bright flowers.	Strong pinks can be sensuous, even erotic. Suggest luxury.

Left: Emil Nolde's brooding sea pictures achieve an almost frightening atmosphere by their use of heightened colours, that nevertheless reflect those to be found in nature. Deep blue, purple and yellow set up a violent and threatening contrast.
Below: this group of life studies achieves a feeling of solid realism in the figures, despite the use of apparently "unrealistic" blocks of colour to define the body shapes.

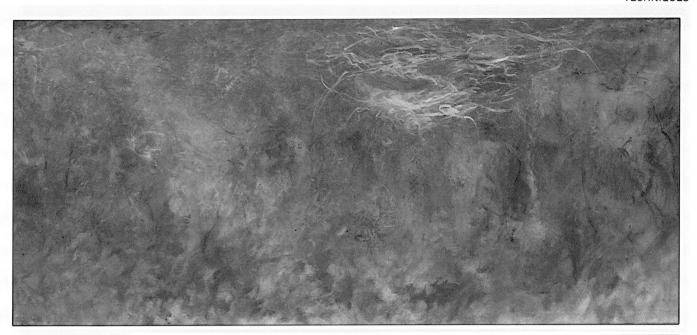

Left: a limited range of colours have been used to create a neutral setting for the almost sculptural shapes within the room, heightening the impact of the black fireback as the focal point. **Above:** the interaction of strong colours has become the real subject of this study of a lilypond. **Right:** a transcription of Degas' painting *After the Bath* has used a heightened colour scheme to place the emphasis on the satisfying unity of shapes that make up the composition.

REFERENCE

Having mastered the basic elements of the art of
oil painting, many people feel tempted to
explore the related craft. On the following pages
you will find alternative materials and methods
of preparing and executing your work. These
recipes for grounds, oil paint and varnishes,
among others, take the art of painting one step
further. Also, the experience to be gained from
preparing homemade materials, experimenting
with them and benefiting from their different
qualities, gives a painter more control and
understanding of the end result.
Interest aside, doing it yourself is always more
economical, although it demands patience to
develop the correct technique. Practice is the
only way to master any of these skills, but do not
get so immersed in working on these aspects
that you divert more time to them than the real
business of painting.

RECIPES AND CANVAS CARE

There are some important safety tips to bear in mind. Keep a set of containers and utensils solely for preparing these mixtures, as most of the ingredients can be harmful if accidentally taken. Keep turps away from a naked flame, and store it in glass bottles or jars, as it will eat through plastic. A useful hint is to stick some gum strip up the outside of a jar and mark it at regular intervals to use as a guide for measuring out quantities for the recipes.

Rabbit skin size

Use rabbit skin granules rather than sheets as they are easier to measure. Put 70g granules into one litre of cold water and leave overnight. Next morning spoon it into a double boiler and warm until dissolved. Do not allow it to boil as it will lose its sealing qualities. Always use lukewarm. More granules can be added if it is too weak. Size will keep for four or five days in the refrigerator and twice as long with the addition of a few drops of vinegar. This recipe makes a large quantity of size which you will need if you intend to prime a number of canvases and panels.

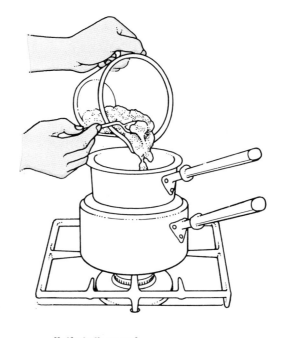

Applying gesso to a board

Size the board and sandpaper lightly. Apply one coat of warm gesso; scrub in with a brush and rub with fingers. If bubbles develop at this stage they will persist to the final coat. Allow to dry thoroughly, or the next coat will lift the previous one. Reheat the gesso and apply the second coat evenly with a varnishing brush from left to right, starting at the edge of the board. Apply up to four coats, depending on the absorbency required, in alternate directions. Allow to dry, rubbing gently with fine sandpaper between each coat. (For a textured surface stipple the final coat with a stiff brush when still damp.) To test when dry put a wet finger on the surface. If the wetness evaporates it is ready; if it is too absorbent. give a final coat of size. Fabric-covered board (see p15) tends to soak up the gesso and will usually need this final coat. Dry at room temperature in daylight.

Making gesso
Chalk ground

1 cup warm size
1 cup whiting (chalk)
1 cup titanium white powder
Sift and mix dry ingredients. Gradually pour in warm size, stirring constantly until it reaches a thin, creamy consistency. This mixture has no flexibility and is only suitable for panels.

Half-chalk ground

Ingredients for chalk ground
$\frac{1}{3}$ cup refined linseed oil
Make up a recipe for chalk ground. Add linseed oil drop by drop, stirring with a spoon trying to prevent the mixture from curdling. The gesso will thicken if allowed to cool. Heat gently over a bowl of hot water to thin. Use on canvas or board.

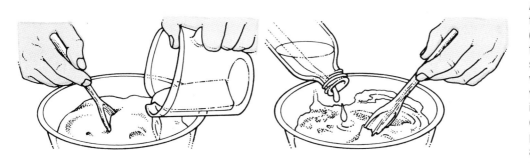

Mediums

Having mastered the use of linseed oil and turps with your paint, try using different oils and vary the proportions you use. Sun-thickened oil is pale, thick and fast drying, stand oil is more viscous and makes the paint more fluid to handle; it is durable but yellows in time. Both these linseed-based oils can be thinned down with linseed oil and turps. Poppy oil is often used in the manufacture of paint. It is a pale, slow-drying oil that does not yellow as much as linseed oil but tends to crack more easily. Damar varnish can be used as a medium (see p108).

A mixture of two parts sun-thickened or stand oil, four parts turps and one part damar varnish is recommended if you want the paint to "stand up" from the canvas.

Beware of adding too much turps or other diluents to the paint as this will thin down the oil and pigment, resulting in a washy appearance. It will also make the paint dry too quickly. However, you could add more than normal when painting on holiday. The painting dries faster and can be worked on each day. Try to find a mixture that allows you to paint at your own pace.

Sun-thickened linseed oil can be made by adding one part water to one part linseed oil in a wide glass container. Keep dust-free covered with a sheet of glass but allow air to pass over the liquid. Place in sunlight and shake once a day for a week. Leave for a few weeks until thick and pour off water.

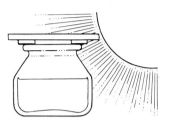

Making oil paints

This is a satisfying, economical and relatively simple operation. The freshly made paints are brighter, and the consistency can be altered according to how much oil is incorporated and whether beeswax is added to give a richer quality. Homemade paints have a stiffer consistency than the commercially prepared paints which, nonetheless in artists' quality, are very good indeed. The proportion of oil to pigment varies greatly (ie Naples yellow requires 15% while Indian yellow requires 100%) so it is best to add the oil gradually until you have the consistency you want. Some pigments can be difficult to grind (such as viridian which will not mix easily with the oil); all are dangerous so wear a mask and avoid the pigments that are most harmful (see 112).

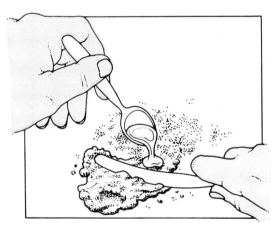

1 Place pigment on a ground glass slab. Add drops of linseed oil and mix with a palette knife.

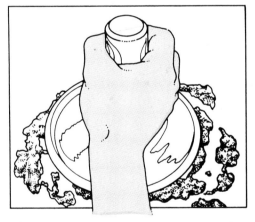

2 Grind in a circular motion with a glass muller until the paint feels quite smooth.

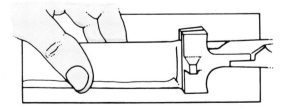

3 Store in airtight jars or fill tubes with a palette knife and crimp ends together with canvas pliers. Clean the glass slab and muller with turps or white spirit.

Varnishing

A painting does not dry thoroughly for nine to twelve months, depending on the thickness of the paint. It should be allowed to dry naturally in daylight before varnishing or it will develop a cloudy "bloom". Heavy-handed varnishing can change the surface of the painting, giving it a dark, glossy sheen which may not be desired; it will, if done properly however, act as a protection against dirt, moisture and temperature and prevent pictures from losing their freshness and colour. There is a wide choice of commercially prepared products as well as recipes for homemade "picture" or "finishing" varnishes that have different properties affecting the matt/gloss qualities and permanence. Damar picture varnish gives a low gloss, copal dries hard to a high gloss, synthetic varnish is reliable and will not yellow, and beeswax is useful as a second varnish to reduce the glossy finish of other varnishes. NB Retouching varnish is only a temporary picture varnish, but it will also bring up sunken patches of paint which occur naturally when working on a picture over a long period.

Applying varnish

Varnish on a dry day, in a dust-free room using a dry brush, having dusted the painting front and back. Pour the varnish into a shallow container and leave in a warm place for half an hour to drive off the moisture. Lie the painting flat. Apply one coat of varnish evenly with a fine-haired brush in 10cm squares. Allow to dry overnight. A higher gloss will be achieved with more coats. For a matt surface gently rub on beeswax varnish with a cloth or brush and polish off with a soft cloth or piece of silk. Dabbing the still tacky picture varnish with a large, bushy brush will also give a matt effect. Varnish takes at least one month to dry. Spraying is not recommended, but if it is done, test for a fine spray (dilute with turps if necessary); make sure it does not drip, and apply three light coats.

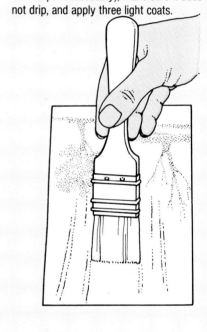

Making varnish

Damar varnish Use one part gum damar to three parts turps. Tie the resin in a muslin bag and suspend in the turps. Allow to stand for two days and strain the impurities through another piece of muslin. Store in an airtight bottle. To make damar medium use on part gum damar, one part turps, using the same method.

Beeswax varnish Use one part beeswax to one part turps. Break up beeswax into small pieces and add to warm turps in a glass jar sitting in hot water (not near a naked flame). Stir until dissolved. Store in an airtight jar. Beeswax should be employed as a second varnish; it can also be used as a painting medium if diluted with more turps.

Cleaning and repairs

The best way to avoid cleaning and repairing your painted canvases is, obviously, to take good care of them. Paintings should be hung in a steady room temperature as cold will crack the paint and too much heat will damage both the painting and the joints of the frame. Do not store paintings in the dark as this will cause the oils to darken over the years. Dust pictures frequently, front and back, to prevent the build-up of dirt. This is particularly important if the picture is not framed behind glass.

Minor repairs and cleaning can be done at home but it is best to leave anything serious to an experienced restorer. Varnished paintings can be cleaned lightly but take great care as water can do a lot of harm to a canvas. Try cleaning a painting with the middle of some newly baked white bread; rub small pieces over the surface and discard when dirty. Do not attempt any repairs on work other than your own and don't try to clean any recently painted or varnished surfaces.

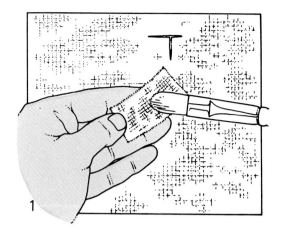

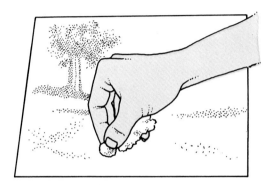

Cleaning To clean varnished paintings wipe gently in a circular action with cotton wool dipped in a little mild soapy water and dry with a cloth. Cleaning emulsions are safer to use. Spread on with cotton wool and wipe off after two minutes; repeat if necessary. Try cleaning with bread (see above).

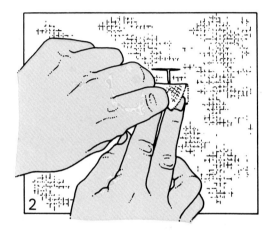

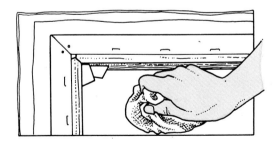

Removing bulges Place the canvas face down on waxed paper. Sponge the bulge with warm water. As the canvas dries the bulge will tighten. Allow to dry naturally. If the canvas appears a little slack, drive in the wedges.

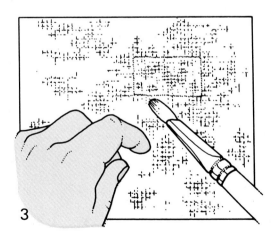

Repairs Attempt nothing larger than a minor tear. **1** Cut a small piece of raw canvas of the same quality that will just cover the tear. Size it and the tear. **2** Lay the patch in place, making sure that the grain lies in the same direction, and smooth down with the finger. **3** Size again and allow to dry. Turn over and carefully prime the crack on the front of the canvas.

FRAMING

Choose a frame carefully, in proportion to the size of the picture, and right for the subject, colour and style. To make a frame yourself requires some simple DIY equipment. Corner clamps provide a short-cut to ensure that the corners are true. You can buy ready-made mouldings; wood types can be cut at home, but composition mouldings are best machine-cut. A painting can be glazed if it has not been varnished, although it will reflect badly if hung in the wrong light. Separate the glass from the painting with a strip of wood or thick card mounted between the two. This "fillet" is invisible if narrower than the frame, or you can have it visible. Avoid non-reflecting glass; it tends to distort the image.

Cross-section of a moulding

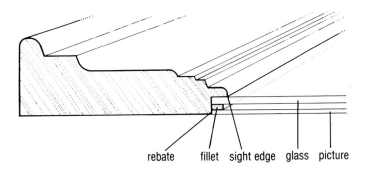

rebate   fillet   sight edge   glass   picture

Making a frame

1 Measure all four sides of the frame. Mark out the lengths on the sight edge of the moulding. Cut each piece at an accurate 45° angle in a mitre box with a fine-tooth saw, on the outside of the mark.

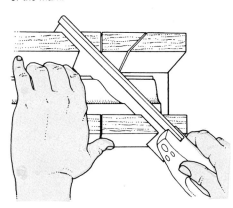

3 Check frame is a true rectangle with a tri-square. Weight down under a board on a flat surface. When dry turn frame over and lay painting on rebate (you should back a panel with hardboard). Tap in pins to secure.

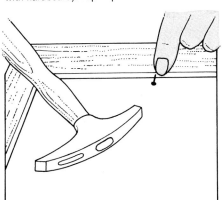

2 Assemble an L with one short and one long side. Hold one piece in a vice and line up the other accurately. Drill holes, apply glue, and hammer in panel pins. Assemble opposite L and then two Ls together.

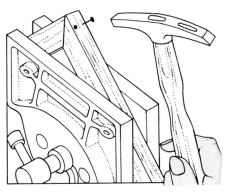

4 If you have backed the painting seal the crack between the board or stretcher and the frame with brown gummed strip. Fix screw rings one third down on the back. use wire or nylon cord to hang the painting.

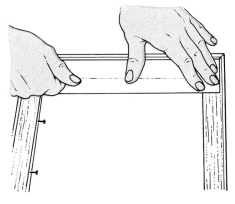

Decorating the frame

To make the most of a natural wood frame such as oak or pine, sand to a smooth finish and apply a white wax polish. Staining will accentuate the grain. Use gesso as an undercoat or as a finished surface.

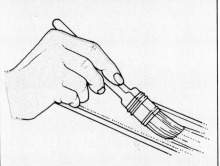

Gesso Apply two or three coats (see p106). Mix some dry pigment with titanium white and warm size. Brush on thinly and quickly while still warm. Rub in with a cloth. When dry polish with a soft cloth.

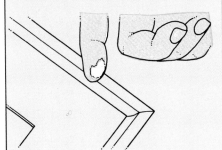

Gold For a gilt finish without using gold leaf use a "gold" paste (such as Goldfinger or Treasure Gold). Apply sparingly with a finger or soft cloth and buff up. Also use to disguise damaged gold leaf.

STORAGE

Materials

Canvas can be bought in bulk, rolled up loosely and stored in an airy room; it will keep for years in the right conditions. Ready-primed canvas can also be bought in bulk but test it first for proneness to yellowing. To do this, cut samples of various qualities in two; mark them and hang one in bright light, the other in the dark for three months. Do not fold primed or raw canvas.

Paint does not keep in prime condition indefinitely so do not buy in bulk unless you use large quantities and do not be tempted to buy paints reduced in a sale since they will probably be old. When you have finished painting for the day, squeeze the end of the tubes to get rid of the air, wipe the threads of the tube and cap and screw tight (see p21). Keep the labels clean so that you can identify the colours.

Brushes should be washed after every painting session (see p19). Never allow paint to dry on the brush and don't soak a brush in turpentine above the metal ferrule. Brushes can be stood in a pot, bristles up, but if putting them away for some time, make sure they are quite clean and dry and store them flat on corrugated cardboard in a box with a lid, protected with a few mothballs.

Finished work

Paintings should be stored flat if they are not going to be hung and it is best to take them off their stretchers and pin them to sturdy composition board. If you are transporting an unframed or unstretched painted canvas, sandwich it between two pieces of board and tie together with string. For a more temporary measure prop up stretched paintings and boards against a wall, facing inwards; separate the mouldings with piece of cardboard. Take a strip of wood to the floor about half a metre from the wall to stop them sliding. If you have to roll up a painted canvas wrap it around a large cylinder, paint side out, to avoid cracking the surface.

Sketches used as preliminary studies for oil painting should be fixed if they are charcoal or soft pastel, pencil or conté, or interleaved with tissue paper and then stored in a plan chest or portfolio. Keep all your sketches, however insignificant you feel they are. They will be useful for reference and future compositions.

Dangerous materials

The basic rule must be to respect your materials – most are harmful to some degree. Fix drawings in a well-ventilated room; do not mixed pigments in the kitchen or any raw materials in cooking utensils; do not chew the handles of your brushes. Most important of all, do not allow children in your studio alone.

Pigments: dry pigments are dangerous to inhale. Some are poisonous, especially the cadmiums and chromes. Flake white is white lead; this should be used only as paint from the tube as it is highly poisonous; be sure to scrub your hands and fingernails thoroughly after using it.

Turpentine: store in the dark in a glass container (it will eat through plastic) and don't have it near a naked flame. Those allergic to turpentine should use white spirit as a substitute.

Varnish: natural and synthetic resins are highly inflammable and the fumes should not be inhaled.

Metric conversion table

Weight

28g	1oz
70g	$2\frac{1}{2}$oz
114g	4oz
227g	8oz
454g	1lb
1kg	$2\frac{1}{4}$lb

Capacity

14ml	$\frac{1}{2}$fl oz
28ml	1fl oz
284ml	10fl oz ($\frac{1}{2}$ UK pt)
454ml	16fl oz(1 US pt)
568ml	20fl oz (1 UK pt)
1l	$1\frac{3}{4}$ UK pt (2 US pt)

Size

25mm (2.5cm)	1in
305mm (30.5cm)	12in (1ft)
914mm (91.4cm)	36in (1yd)
1000mm (1m)	39in
1524mm (1m 52.4cm)	60in (5ft)

GLOSSARY

Aerial perspective
See Perspective.

Alla prima
Finishing the painting in one go.

Chiaroscuro
(Italian, meaning light-dark.) The play of contrasted light and shade.

Complementary colours
Any colour is complementary to the colour with which it contrasts most strongly, as red with green, yellow with violet, blue with orange. Complementary colours occur opposite each other on the conventional colour wheel.

Cool colours
See Temperature.

Counterchange
Interaction of contrasting tones or colours. See page 48.

Earth colours
Pigments obtained from clay or minerals rather than chemicals, they are less intense than synthetic colours.

Gesso
Chalk- or gypsum-based ground applied to a board or panel, producing a smooth white surface.

Glaze
Transparent or semi-transparent layer of oil paint to modify the underlying colour.

Ground
The prepared surface on which the painting is painted, either a layer of paint (sometimes tinted) or, in the *alla prima* method, the white primed canvas.

Hatching
Shading or filling in with lines roughly parallel.

Hue
Chromatic value of a colour (as opposed to its tonal value).

Impasto
The build up of thick, opaque oil paint.

Key
The general range of a set of colours. A painting has a high key of colour when its dominant values are bright and its hues are light.

Local colour
The intrinsic colour of a form, disregarding the effects of light on it.

Life painting
Painting from direct observation of the model.

Medium
1 The material or technique of a work of art.
2 The binder in which pigment is held and hence the kind of paint—oil, tempera, acrylic.
3 Oil, wax or varnish added to oil paint to change its consistency.

Modelling
The description of form by creating the illusion of solidity.

Modulation
The gradual change of colours or tones.

Monochrome
Strictly, in one colour; usually, in black and white, or brown or grey without colour.

Negative shape
A term applied to the abstract shapes seen in the space between forms. The form may be called a positive shape.

Palette
The board on which the artist arranges and mixes his colours; hence, also the range of his colours.

Passage
Part, area or excerpt of a painting (as if from a book).

Perspective
Conveyance or suggestion of distance in painting. Linear perspective involves the use of a vanishing point towards which receding horizontal lines converge. Aerial perspective is the suggestion of distance by a tone, for instance using lighter and cooler colours as they approach the horizon.

Pigment
The colouring substance in paint (as opposed to the medium or binder); simply colour.

Plane
Face or surface, understood as being flat and of two dimensions. An object can be painted as if it consisted of several planes or faces meeting at

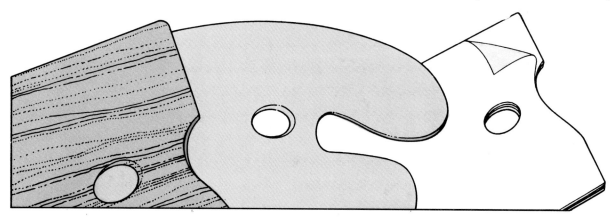

different angles. Also used to describe areas of a composition, in the same way that foreground, middle- and background are defined. The picture plane is the surface of a painting.

Plein air
A painting executed in the landscape to capture the impression of the open air.

Positive shape
See Negative shape.

Primary colours
Red, yellow and blue are the primary colours, from which the secondary colours derive by mixing: red with yellow creates orange, yellow with blue creates green, blue with red creates violet. Mixtures of secondary with primary colours create tertiary colours.

Primer
The first white layer, emulsion, gesso, oil or acrylic on which all subsequent layers of paint are applied.

Reflected colour
The colour of a form as modified by the light and colours around it (as opposed to local colour).

Restating
The process of changing and altering as one paints.

Saturated colour
Colour of full intensity with no white added.

Scumbling
The overlaying of opaque broken colour allowing the underpainting to be partially lost.

Secondary colours
See Primary colours.

Size
Glue size (derived from animal hide or gelatin) is used as a surface preparation on canvas or board before priming.

Stain
A wash of colour that is absorbed by the ground.

Still life
Painting objects, usually close up.

Stippling
The application of paint in flecks with the point of the brush rather than in continuous strokes; or any similar dotted effect.

Support
Stretcher and canvas, wood panel, board, or other material on which to paint.

Temperature
A quality of colour. Red is the hottest colour, blue the coolest. Optically warmer colours seem to advance and cooler colours recede.

Tertiary colours
See Primary colours.

Tone
Degree or quality of light to dark shade, hence dark tones, light tones, mid- or half-tones. Colours also may be dark or light and therefore possess a tonal value.

"Tonking"
(from the English painter Henry Tonks.) Technique of removing paint by covering an area with a material that absorbs most of the excess oil and surface paint, then drawing it off to leave an image.

Tooth
Weave or texture of a canvas or other support (first used of paper).

Underpainting
The initial layers or build-up of a painting, laid over the ground. Though often invisible in the finished work, it may crucially affect its colours.

Value
Quality or degree of a tone or colour. A colour, such as red, may change its value and become, for instance, orange; or a colour or monochrome area may have a certain tonal value, on a scale between light and dark. Where the term occurs without a context, it generally means simply tone.

Vanishing point
In perspective, a point on the horizon towards which lines receding into depth converge.

Warm colours
See Temperature.

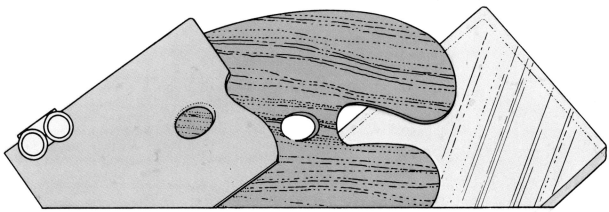

INDEX

absorbency, surface, 35
advancing colour, 43
aerial perspective, 80
alla prima style, 33
  definition, 114
alterations, 66-7
animals, 96-9
  in a landscape, 98
Armfield, Diana, 69
artificial light, colour
  temperature, 41

balance of shapes, 52-3
beeswax varnish, 108
birds, 96-9
blockboard supports, 10-11
boards, 10-11
  applying gesso to, 106
  preparing, 10
  priming, 16-17
  sizing, 14-15
  types, 11
boats, 91
brights, 18
bristle brushes, 18-19
brush marks, 32-3
  absorbency of the surface, 35
  angled strokes, 33
  applying thick paint, 33
  applying thin paint, 33
  bold strokes, 33
  impasto, 34
  scumbling, 34
  small touches, 32
brushes, 18-19
  breaking in, 18
  cleaning, 19
  holding, 27
  range, 18-19
  storage, 112
  using, 32-3
  worn, 18
buildings, 92-5

calico canvas, 9
canvas, 8-9
  buying, 8
  choosing, 8
  format, 54
  pre-stretchers, 8
  priming, 16-17
  sizing, 14-15

  storage, 112
  stretching, 12-13
  types, 9
canvases
  care of, 109
  framing, 110-11
  repair of, 109
  storage, 112
cardboard supports, 10
Cézanne, Paul, 33
chiaroscuro, definition, 114
cleaning
  brushes, 18-19
  painted canvases, 109
  palettes, 23
clothing, in figure painting, 74
clouds, 87
colour
  advancing, 43
  associations, 100
  behaviour of, 42
  chromatic palette, 100
  classical palette, 100
  complementary, 39, 114
  cool, 41
  cool palette, 100
  definition, 42
  emotional response, 100
  exercises, 46-7
  and expression, 100-3
  glazing, 67
  hues, 39, 42, 114
  interaction, 42
  keys, 39
  in the landscape, 86
  modulation, 51
  observed, 46-7
  primary, 115
  receding, 43
  recording, 83
  reflected, definition, 115
  saturated, definition, 115
  shades, 39
  temperature, 41, 115
  tints, 39, 42, 115
  tonal painting, 40-1
  tonal values, 36-7
  warm, 41
  warm palette, 100
  weights, 62
  wheel, 36-7
complementary colours, 39
  definition, 114

composition
  animal paintings, 97
  balanced structure, 62
  depth, 80-1
  development, 64-5
  flower painting, 69
  format, 54
  found, 56
  Golden Section, 55
  harmony, 55-7
  imposed, 57
  looking at, 62-3
  proportion, 55-7
  scale, 80-1
conversion tables, 112
cool colours, 41, 100
Carot, Jean Baptiste Camille,
  Island of San Bartolomeo, 94
cotton supports, 8, 9
counterchange, 48
  definition, 114
damar varnish, 107
dangerous materials, storage, 112
dark colours, applying, 35
daylight, colour temperature, 41
Degas, Edgar
  After the Bath, 103
  Combing the Hair, 55
depth, 80-1
  creating, 50-1
diagonals, 55
dippers, 22
distance, 80-1
domestic animals, 96
drawings
  pen and ink, 83
  pencil, 58, 83
  for portraits, 76
  underdrawings, 60

earth colours, definition, 114
easels, 24-5
  adjusting, 25
  extras, 25
edges
  restating, 67
  of shapes, 51
egg emulsion primers, 16
emotional responses, to colours, 100
emulsion primers, 16
equipment
  brushes, 18-19
  easels, 24-5

knives, 22
palettes, 22-3

fat paints, 60
feathers, 98
figure painting, 72-3
clothing in, 74
colour, 74-5
form, 74-5
portraits, 76-9
preliminary drawings, 76
selecting a pose, 77
self-portraits, 75
shape, 73
squaring up, 73
tone, 73
filberts, 18
fish, scales, 99
flat shapes, 50
flats, 18
flowers
arranging, 70
composition, 69
painting, 69-71
foliage, 87
form, 50-1
format, 54
framing, 110-11
fur, 98
Gainsborough, Thomas, 45
gesso
applying, 106
definition, 114
frames, 111
making, 106
primers, 17
gilding frames, 111
glass, reflections, 93
glazes, 34
applying, 67
definition, 114
Golden Section, 55
grids, making, 47
ground
definition, 114
half-chalk, 106
toned, 44-5

half-chalk ground, making, 106
hardboard supports, 10-11
sizing, 14-15
harmony, 55-7

diagonals, 55
found composition and, 56
Golden Section, 55
imposed composition and, 57
hatching, definition, 114
hessian, 8
hues, 39, 42
definition, 114

impasto, 34
definition, 114
interacton of colour, 42
inverted views, 63

jute canvas, 9

keys, colour, 39
definition, 114
knives
building up with, 35
impasto, 34
painting, 22
palette, 22
scraping down, 66
using, 34

landscapes
animals in, 98
building the picture, 86
clouds, 87
colour, 86
finishing touches, 86
foliage, 87
oil sketches, 85
painting, 84-9
response to subject, 84
selecting subjects, 84
sketching, 82, 84-5
skies, 87
starting, 84
tonal range, 83
trees, 87
working to time limits, 84-5
lean paints, 60
lettering, 93
life painting, definition, 114
light colours, applying, 35
lighting, 26
colour temperature, 41
still life, 68

line, 48-9
counterchange, 48
painting in, 49
qualities of, 49
linear perspective, 80
linen canvas, 8, 9
linseed oil
in mediums, 21
in primers, 17
sun-thickened, 107
local colour, definition, 114

mahogany supports, 10
masks, 58
materials, 6-27
boards, 10-11
brushes, 18-19
canvas, 8-9, 12-13
dangerous, 112
easels, 24-5
knives, 22
mediums, 20-1
paints, 20-1
palettes, 23-4
primers, 16-17
size, 14-15
supports, 8-13
Matisse, Henri, *The Pink Nude,* 48
mediums, 20-1
definition, 114
making, 107
metric conversion tables, 112
modelling, definition, 114
modulation, definition, 114
Monet, Claude, *Two Women on the Beach,* 56
monochrome, definition, 114
moulding, frames, 111
muslin supports, 8

negative shapes, 52
definition, 114
newspaper, 'tonking', 66, 115
Nolde, Emil, 101

observation, 58
oil board, 10-11

painting knives, 22
using, 34

paintings
care of, 109
repair of, 109
storage, 112
paints, 20-1
applying thick, 33
applying thin, 33
caring for, 21
laying out, 37
making, 107
removing excess oil, 21
selecting for the palette, 37
setting on the palette, 37
storage, 112
stuck caps, 21
underpainting, 60
palette
chromatic, 100
classical, 100
cool, 100
definition, 114
warm, 100
palette knives, 22
scraping down, 66
using, 34, 35
palettes, 22-3
cleaning, 23
easel rests, 25
holding, 23
making, 22-3
selecting paints for, 37
setting, 37
paper supports, 10
passage, definition, 114
pen and ink drawings, 83
pencil drawings and sketches, 59, 83
perspective
aerial, 80
creating depth, 80
definition, 114
line and, 49
linear, 80
pets, 96
pigments, storage, 112
definition, 114
Pisarro, Camille, *View from My Window, Eragny,* 38
plane, definition, 114-15
plein air, definition, 115
plywood supports, 10-11
poppy oil, 107
portraits
painting, 76-9

preliminary drawings, 76
selecting a pose, 77
self-portraits, 75
positive shapes, 52
definition, 115
preparations, 26-7
primary colours, definition, 115
primed canvas, stretching, 13
primer, definition, 115
priming, 16-17
proportion, 55-7
diagonals, 55
found composition and, 56
imposed composition and, 57

rabbit skin size, 14
recipe, 106
radial easels, 24, 25
receding colour, 43
recipes, 106-7
reflected colour, definition, 115
reflected views, 63
reflections
glass, 93
water, 90, 93
repainting, 66-7
repairing, painted canvases, 109
reptiles, scales, 99
restating, 66-7
definition, 115
rhythm of painting, 27
ripples, water, 90
Rubens, Sir Peter Paul, 45
Ruisdael, Jacob, *Landscape with Ruins,* 57

sable brushes, 18-19
saturated colour, definition 115
scale, 80-1
buildings, 92
scraping down, 66
scumbling, 34
definition, 115
seascapes, 88-9, 90-1
self-portraits, 75
shades, 39
shadows, 51, 61
shape, 50-1
animal paintings, 97
balance of, 52-3
complex and simple, 53
creating depth, 50-1

defined by line, 49
edges, 51, 67
flat, 50
format, 54
modulated, 50
negative, 52, 114
passive and active, 52
positive, 52, 115
small and large, 53
space between, 52
three dimensional representation, 51
size
definition, 115
rabbit skin, 106
sizing, 14-15
sketchbooks, 82-3
choosing, 82
sketches, 61
landscapes, 82, 84-5
pen and ink, 83
pencil, 59, 83
storage, 112
sketching easels, 24
skies, 87
squaring up, 73
stain, definition, 115
stains, building up, 35
still life, 58
background, 68
composing, 68
definition, 115
depth, 68
light, 68
placing objects, 68
stippling, 34
definition, 115
storage, 112
brushes, 112
canvas, 112
dangerous materials, 112
materials, 112
paint, 112
paintings, 112
pigments, 112
sketches, 112
turpentine, 112
street signs, 93
stretchers, 8, 12-13
structure, 62
studio easels, 24
studios, 26
subjects
composing a still life, 68

figures, 72-9
flowers, 69-71
framing, 58
investigating, 58
landscapes, 84-9
looking at, 58
pencil sketches, 59
seascapes, 88-9, 90-1
sun-thickened linseed oil,
making, 107
Sundeala supports, 10-11
supports
alternative, 8
boards, 10-11
canvas, 8, 12-13
definition, 115
priming, 16-17
sizing, 14-15
symmetry, 53

table easels, 24
temperature, 41
definition, 115
texture
animal paintings, 97, 98-9
canvas, 9
created by line, 49
three dimensions, representing, 51
tilt board easels, 24
tinted grounds, 44-5
tints, 39, 42
Titian, *Bacchus and Ariadne,* 31
tone, 95
definition, 115
drawings, 83
tonal painting, 40-1, 73
tonal range in landscapes, 83
tonal scale, 36
weights, 62
toned grounds, 44-5
'tonking', 66
definition, 115
tooth, definition, 115
towns, 92-5
trees, 87
turpentine, 21
storage, 112

underdrawings, 60
underpainting, 45, 60
definition, 115

value, definition, 115
Van Gogh, Vincent, 33
vanishing point,
definition, 115
varnish
applying, 108
beeswax, 108
making, 108
storage, 112
viewpoints, 58

warm colours, 41, 100
definition, 115
water
reflections, 90, 93
ripples, 90
seascapes, 88-9, 90-1
workrooms, 26

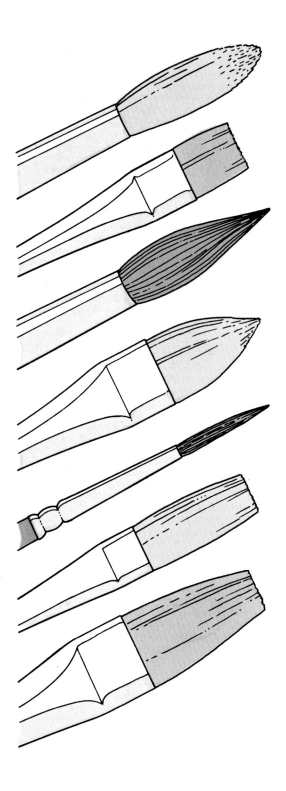

PICTURE CREDITS